Learning Analytics for Achieving Quality Assurance in Higher Learning Institutions

This book explores Learning Analytics (LA) programs and practices in Malaysia, including the underlying forces, dilemmas and policy challenges for quality assurance (QA) in higher education institutions (HEIs).

The chapters in this book provide a comprehensive discussion of trends in academic QA in higher education. It articulates a combination of theoretical issues and empirical analysis and offers a comprehensive guide to stakeholders in management and faculty on LA implementation in HEIs, where the model proposed in this book can be used to pave the way for successful LA initiatives. LA is an emerging multidisciplinary technological practice with the ultimate goal of facilitating effective learning to improve students' achievement at the tertiary level.

The LA model of QA recommended in this book is an essential guide for any faculty or managers in higher education or researchers in higher education and LA.

Soo Mang Lim is a lecturer in ELM Graduate School, HELP University Malaysia, and the head of the Department of the School of Hospitality and Tourism, HELP University Malaysia.

Husaina Banu Kenayathulla is an associate professor in the Department of Educational Management, Planning and Policy, Faculty of Education, University of Malaya, Malaysia.

Routledge Research in Higher Education

The Layered Landscape of Higher Education
Capturing Curriculum, Diversity and Cultures of Learning in Australia
Edited by Margaret Kumar, Supriya Pattanayak and Nish Belford

Authority, Passion, and Subjected-Centered Teaching
A Christian Pedagogical Philosophy
Christopher J. Richmann

Experiential Learning and Community Partnerships for Sustainable Development
A Foundational Model for Climate Action
Mara Huber, Michael Jabot, and Christina Heath

Philosophical Adventures in African Higher Education
Cultivating Doctoral Encounters within Democratic Citizenship Education
Edited by Yusef Waghid

Developing Feedback Literacy for Academic Journal Peer Review
Narratives from Researchers in Education and Applied Linguistics
Edited by Sin Wang Chong and Aurora Lixinhao Gao

Exploring Research Impact in Academia and Why it Matters
Perspectives on the Public Good and the Role of Research in Society
Andy Phippen and Louise Rutt

Learning Analytics for Achieving Quality Assurance in Higher Learning Institutions
Malaysian Perspectives for Global Insights
Soo Mang Lim and Husaina Banu Kenayathulla

For more information about this series, please visit: www.routledge.com/Routledge-Research-in-Higher-Education/book-series/RRHE

Learning Analytics for Achieving Quality Assurance in Higher Learning Institutions

Malaysian Perspectives for Global Insights

Soo Mang Lim and Husaina Banu Kenayathulla

LONDON AND NEW YORK

First published 2025
by Routledge
4 Park Square, Milton Park, Abingdon, Oxon OX14 4RN

and by Routledge
605 Third Avenue, New York, NY 10158

Routledge is an imprint of the Taylor & Francis Group, an informa business

British Library Cataloguing-in-Publication Data
A catalogue record for this book is available from the British Library

ISBN: 978-1-032-95364-9 (hbk)
ISBN: 978-1-032-95365-6 (pbk)
ISBN: 978-1-003-58452-0 (ebk)

DOI: 10.4324/9781003584520

Typeset in Times New Roman
by Apex CoVantage, LLC

Contents

Preface

Dramatic shifts brought about by globalization, technological innovation and data-driven decision-making practices are immensely reflected in the landscape of 21st-century higher education. Learning Analytics (LA) is an emerging multidisciplinary, technological practice with the ultimate goal of facilitating effective learning to improve students' achievement at the tertiary level. Hence, this book is a critical contributor to unveiling the importance of LA to students' learning processes and learning outcomes from a global perspective, particularly in relation to achieving quality assurance (QA) in higher learning institutions in Malaysia.

The book showcases contributions from scholars, researchers and practitioners who have a deep understanding of LA and education management, reflecting the perspectives of management teams and faculty members. The authors of this book are inspired by two significant factors. First, given the growing importance of LA in students' learning processes and learning outcomes, it remains imperative for higher education institutions (HEIs) in Malaysia to understand the contribution of LA towards impacting students' learning processes and outcomes. Second, the implementation of LA could elevate the QA standards in higher education.

Chapter 1 offers some definitions and explanations on how LA offers various kinds of computational intervention for tracking students' data and behavior and providing quantifiable feedback to both instructors and students at the program level. That has become a new phenomenon in reflection of technology integration that has led many HEIs today in preparing students for continuous lifetime learning in a world filled with intricacies and uncertainties. In addition, scholars and researchers have also hailed that the effective use of "Big Data" and LA is a critical component of a digital learning strategy to personalize instruction for more students, particularly to increase/achieve students' graduate attributes. By seamlessly integrating Artificial Intelligence (AI) with established learning theories, scholars and researchers can embark on a more comprehensive exploration of how this powerful combination can revolutionize student learning. Despite the point that LA is relatively new in the research field as well as professional practices in higher education today, especially in Malaysia, the authors are inspired to find out to what extent LA can be a tool to improvise students' learning processes and learning outcomes for QA despite the barriers such as strategic direction, human adaptability to cultural change, technological and infrastructural support, teaching and learning policies and management, as well as ethical use of data.

Chapter 2 examines the development of learning theories and how LA can be integrated into pedagogical frameworks to achieve maximum gain to support students' learning. Considering how LA is measured based on knowledge, pedagogies and assessment, students' learning processes is reflected in the review of LA and its benefits, and students' learning outcomes is predominantly reflected in the review of QA. Hence, all other aspects in relation to the specific issues concerned were investigated, focusing on LA based on QA of higher education in Malaysia from a global perspective. A conceptual model was employed to inductively explore the theoretical framework on LA and its benefits from the perspective of knowledge and issues in students' learning processes and outcomes, learning theories and their implementation; QA from the perspective of academic QA and QA of HEIs of Malaysia; stakeholders from the perspective of management team and faculty members; as well as the challenges in value embeddedness and the emerging policies and directions of Malaysian higher education. The researcher has dedicated a portion of the chapter to exploring the connection between LA and personalized learning through AI. Examples are provided of how AI algorithms can be designed to align with the established theories.

In Chapter 3, with the understanding of how knowledge is built, the authors have a better understanding of the effective use of data in LA as one of the critical components to increase students' graduate attributes. The nine current issues on students' learning processes and learning outcomes, reviewed include rising cost of learning leading to incompletion of programs; learning digital literacy to integrate formal and informal learning approaches; knowledge management; 21st-century skills; transfer of knowledge; response to new methods of teaching and curriculum; response to quality teaching; capacity of teachers for learning reform; and technology infrastructure and ethical use of data.

The following chapter discuss the interventions designed to deliver the right information to the appropriate students at the optimal time, with the goal of improving student performance. Feedback is crucial for learning and achievement, as it provides valuable insights into both the learning outcomes and the effectiveness of our ongoing and immediate efforts, such as interventions. Whether age, education level, academic load, and the term of enrolment were predictive of academic performance were discussed. Finally, the authors explored if LA can be done ethically. Issues on privacy, individuality, autonomy and discrimination were discussed, including solidifying and legitimating the LA process. Moreover, values include boosting retention rate (identifying struggling students earlier); performance tracking to increase learning success rate; adjustment of students' own path and pace of learning; types of learning-tailored instruction; and real-time feedback. Besides, LA is a platform to continuously upskill academics and enhance educational research. Well, the focus of instructors and institutional concerns are different. LA will benefit only if it is implemented correctly with the full participation of all required stakeholders. Furthermore, implementation challenges such as the value of LA and its embeddedness for success in the context of students, faculty and management must also be addressed. In light of this, this chapter discusses challenges in strategic direction and change and leadership and culture.

In Chapter 5, the authors elucidate the significance of LA in the curriculum content and delivery of higher education as outlined in the Malaysia Education Blueprint 2015–2025 (Higher Education), particularly in addressing the demands and transformations associated with the Fourth Industrial Revolution (4IR) and its implications. QA is the means by which an institution guarantees that the standard and values of the scholastic provision are being sustained and improved with confidence and certainty. The QA system of the country in the context of globalization, internationalization and transformation in redressing the environment of learning and teaching must become accustomed to the shifting surroundings. Through the lens of LA, to what extent can the guidelines on criteria and standards of codes of practice for program accreditation (COPPA) and codes of practice for institutional audit (COPIA) be achieved accordingly to fit their distinct purpose? In this background, the chapter reviews the program's aims and objectives, including learning outcomes; the implementation of curriculum assessment methods/strategies; and learning and teaching strategies.

The final chapter unveils the "importance of understanding LA to students' learning processes and learning outcomes in achieving QA of higher education within the Malaysian higher education landscape", specifically in the context of students' achievement, viability and the sustainability of transformation. In the context of achieving quality assurance (QA), LA plays a crucial role in evaluating the effectiveness of educational interventions and fostering institutional transformation. Aligned with the Malaysia Education Blueprint (2015–2025) (Higher Education), the implementation of LA can be considered a transformative change program. To ensure successful implementation, it is essential to consider the potential impact on institutional diversity and align LA practices not only with the national QA system but also with international standards. By investigating LA as a process of ongoing evaluation, this research aims to contribute to a deeper understanding of its role in driving educational improvement and fostering a more effective and equitable learning environment.

The chapters in this book collectively provide a timely overview drawn based on the impactful critical success factors. The inter-relationships between LA and QA have become the focus, which include students' academic experience, successful implementation of LA and strategic direction.

LA can be made successful toward achieving QA with the proposed mechanism of a determinative approach with the subset of three focal entities. In recent research, AI has been used to predict student performance by analyzing learning activities. Additionally, LA Tools offer insights for evidence-based decision-making in higher education. We hope that they will embrace LA on the way to future sustainability of QA in higher education, especially in the aspect of students' academic experiences and achievements in higher education. Ultimately, this synthesizes effective teaching and learning on the technological platform, such as online learning, where teaching pedagogies, adoption of technology, student workload, student assessments and other indicators come into place. I wish this book would be a comprehensive guide on LA implementation in HEIs, so the model can be used to pave the way for a successful LA initiative.

Overview

The implementation of LA for achieving QA is a journey. This book aims to show the comprehensive perilous triumph elements that enable a more justifiable implementation of LA for accomplishing QA in higher learning institutions. Furthermore, it showcases how AI can further enhance data analysis, personalization and the overall effectiveness of LA practices. As LA is still a new technology in the education environment in Malaysia, it is important to investigate LA in the local context before applying it to the HEIs nationwide. Above all, the conceptualization of issues on this new phenomenon and hence the direction for HEIs would inform HEI leaders, faculty and other stakeholders on the extent to which LA achieves QA and beyond, including the implementation of LA initiatives.

On the whole, LA has yet to redeem its promises fully. On that notion, the deployment of LA projects through a substantial number of strategies (even simultaneously) is indeed crucial, upon which policies are to be laid in more detailed themes. The incorporation of a broad vision of academic excellence, good judgment of investment potential and the full engagement of faculties are also critical. In view that managing HEIs is a very complicated task, institutions would require buy-in not only from the faculty but also from the leadership of staff and management and even the students themselves. All stakeholders must be clear on what problem they are striving to resolve, how glitches can be explained cumulatively and who can aid to unravel the snags.

Educators have to establish that they are dependable caretakers of respectable-value higher education while simultaneously functioning as reliable providers of good-quality higher education in intricate situations with various stakeholders, each with their own anticipations (government, management, faculties, students and parents). To accomplish performance in teaching and learning in accordance with the National Higher Education Strategic Plan (MOE, 2015), the attainment of Excellence in Phase 3 and Beyond 2020 Glory and Sustainability in Phase 4 of the plan may not yet be realized. To enable students to more effectively compete for greater academic achievement, an increase in the efficiency of learning processes has become more stringent, especially in funding constraints faced by private HEIs in Malaysia. Besides technology being an important consideration, human factors, especially the integrated culture in using data and analytics by all LA stakeholders, are paramount to the success of implementation; hence, the proposed mechanism of determinative approach is critical in the long term.

1 The World of Learning Analytics

1.1 Overview

Our world is changing at a dizzying speed every day. Globalization, technology innovation and data-driven decision-making are creating new demands and opportunities. For example, in universities, every interaction of the students with their instructors, library visit or login to their online portal will leave behind a digital footprint. According to Sclater et al. (2016), Learning Analytics (LA) is "the process of using those data to improve learning and teaching". That is, it offers various kinds of computational intervention for tracking students' data and behavior and providing quantifiable feedback to both instructors and students at the program level. This has become a new phenomenon reflecting technology integration, leading many higher education institutions (HEIs) today to prepare students for continuous lifetime learning in a world filled with intricacies and uncertainties by bringing about changes to their teaching and learning processes to ensure students are equipped with knowledge, expertise and personalities (OECD, 2017). Researchers have also hailed that the effective use of "big data" and LA is a critical component of a digital learning strategy to personalize instruction for more students, particularly to increase/achieve students' graduate attributes.

In light of the above, institutional diversity has to be matched not only with the QA system of the country but also across national borders to a certain extent where transformation has to do with rectifying the historical, social and economic disparities in cultures, businesses and the environment of teaching and learning (Chinomona, 2013). To serve the students of today and the future is indeed the mission of all educationalists. Could the future of work be done anywhere and the processing power of computers enable machines to outperform humans across an ever-increasing scope of work? Extrapolating from the current practice of HEIs globally, expectations can be anticipated in significant contributions at the academic level. That includes LA serving as a tool to enhance the effectiveness of QA; as a tool to boost student retention rates, such as enabling the identification of students struggling to cope; and as a tool to access and act upon students' learning outcomes, such as in

DOI: 10.4324/9781003584520-1

a performance tracking system of students, so that students' learning success rate is higher. LA also serves as a mechanism for the adjustment of students' own path and pace of learning; the type of learning-tailored instruction; and real-time formative feedback between students and instructors. Besides, this necessitates continuous upskilling for academics and constant enhancement of educational research so as to integrate LA into "intelligent" curriculum in HEIs (Chinomona, 2013; Dix & Leavesley, 2015).

In contrast to traditional students' learning experiences documented in a collaborative research between Malaysian and Australian universities, the implementation of LA, for instance, is at a relatively early stage in Malaysia (Tasir et al., 2016). However, there is convincing evidence that helps to develop more student-focused provision for higher education utilizing data and tools for continuous improvement. A policy that upholds the fundamental principles of the framework enables practitioners to fulfill their commitments, paving the way for future entrepreneurship opportunities. This includes progressing towards sustainable assurance of quality excellence and benchmarking (Tasir et al., 2016).

According to several literatures, despite the point that LA is relatively new in the research field as well as professional practices in higher education today, especially in Malaysia, QA is often omitted from the past studies that were conducted pertaining to LA as a whole (Thille & Zimmaro, 2017; Buyarski et al., 2017; Pistilli & Arnold, 2010; Clow, 2012; Wong, 2017).

1.2 What Is Learning Analytics?

According to Dziuban et al. (2012), analytics is merely the discipline of rational data scrutiny. Analytics of data can be functional in the area of education with the objective of predicting student success and supporting instructors to know when and how to intervene with a student to reduce his/her failure. This is, LA is the main component of study here. It centers on data from students and their circumstances, which will be utilized to develop learning progression or the learning environment (Siemens & Baker, 2012). As a result, instructors will be informed on how to assist struggling students.

Well, using data to inform instruction is no longer a new thing. Traditionally, teachers have been using informal questioning and other formative assessment techniques such as tests/exams in the classroom to gather information on understanding students. LA instead of online learning/face-to-face learning turned into a more structured form, particularly when learning management systems (LMS) became available, which enabled the search of data for stakeholders (Picciano, 2012; Reyes, 2015). LA then emanated with an amplified volume to augment its capacity to analyze a greater quantity of data, whereas the LMS and student information system were connected to track an enormous amount of data. Big data and Artificial Intelligence (AI) are interconnected, with big data consisting of a large amount of data collected from multiple sources in LA. On the other hand, AI includes algorithms and technologies used for analyzing, interpreting and deriving information so that educational outcomes can be improved. Fahd et al. (2023) introduce a Big Data Analytics Solution (BDAS) designed to enhance student success in higher education by leveraging data from Learning Management Systems (LMS). This innovative approach aims to identify students at risk of failing, enabling timely interventions to improve retention rates.

As complied by Lonn et al. (2017) on its origin, LA's first effort was at the University of Michigan, where its groundwork for the analytics community was laid. Many big U.S. secondary schools initiated reassessment of their long-term exercise of retaining student archives, subsequently utilizing electronic student information systems, which became a practice. The study by Wright et al. (2014) was inspired by Freeman's work in 2007 on the importance of feedback in student learning. The three physics faculty members investigated the performance of students in physics courses, focusing on how the limited functionality of existing data systems hindered their ability to use data effectively for instructional purposes. The study found that the existing data system was limited in its functionality, hindering its use for data-driven instruction. The system lacked integration with other educational tools and struggled to provide meaningful insights into student performance. These limitations highlighted the need for more sophisticated data analytics tools to support faculty members in making informed instructional decisions. They have identified who did better and who did worse. In addition, investigation on the intersection of learning technologies in higher education teaching was done and led by Stephanie and Teasley through a series of studies examining perceptions and aggregated use of the institutional LMS (Lonn et al., 2017). At the University of Michigan, though the early effort was led by faculty, a variety of academic and support staff and also students at all levels needed to be involved in creating a culture of awareness and acceptance for LA to acquire bigger support from the institutional community of scholars, researchers and professionals.

In recent years, LA has become an essential concern in higher education in the technology-enhanced learning and teaching areas. Many researchers have established various methods for implementing LA. Take a pause at this point in time; we need to clarify the distinction between LA missions by the different stages of investigations so that the leaders/faculty of the HEIs are clear and certain what LA projects they want to implement based on the direct types of outcomes expected. Zilvinskis et al. (2017) also wrote that there are 2 separate but interrelated domains of the above mentioned: the work that engages the faculty in improving student learning within individual classes and curriculum (LA) and the more holistic student progress, persistence and completion. Certainly, implementation of LA projects does not only require clear understanding of the type of projects to be implemented; the success and sustainability are also very critical depending on the resources/capacity needed for achieving QA in higher education.

The definition of Learning Analytics (LA) aligns closely with the industry-preferred definition from the International Conference on Learning Analytics (LAK, 2011). According to various sources, including Dix and Leavesley (2015), LA is defined as: "Learning Analytics is the measurement, collection, analysis, and reporting of data about learners and their contexts, for purposes of understanding and optimizing learning and the environments in which it occurs". The main crucial elements involved were clearly data, analysis and actions in processing raw data, such as students' performance grades, which get transformed into analytical insights, and intelligence is added to data using algorithms, and ultimately taking action is the goal of any LA process (LAK, 2011). Besides, LA encompasses the usage of a wide choice of data and methods for analysis, such as numerical tests, predictive models and data visualization models (Arroway et al., 2016). Various stakeholders like students, lecturers, staff, government and experts can then take action on data-compelled analysis.

Furthermore, the area of LA is comparatively new; there are not many theories and models that are impacting the usage of the available data to inform and improve learning and teaching (Elias, 2011). Campbell et al. (2007) suggested a five-stage model for LA on implementation: the first stage is capturing data; the second is reporting of data; the third is to make predictions; the fourth is to act on that prediction; and the last stage is to refine data. Accordingly, researchers would employ techniques to ensure that data is to be stored, and once it is retrieved, researchers must make decisions on how to organize the data to move to the next stage (Campbell, et al., 2007). When data is required to be dealt with in a way that it could be concise or jointed to a functional layout for the end-user viewing, such as a dashboard. Statistical software tools have to be used to handle this large quantity of data (Campbell, et al., 2007; Pardo, 2014). The process of prediction is then carried out centered on the data and commentary concluded in the prior stage, which includes responding to questions that instigated capturing the data in a way that describes what is expected to transpire. The accuracy of the prediction is thus dependent on the use of a reliable model (Campbell, et al., 2007). Once the minute prediction is completed, stakeholders are to take action on that prediction. At this point, Campbell et al. (2007) indicated that, subject to the kind of commentary and prediction formed in the course of the initial phase of the LA procedure, activities should differ for diverse end-users such as students, and the ways to help them differ from one another. As for the refining stage, Baker (2007) and Dron and Anderson (2011) indicated that calling out for the refinement of data makes the model stronger. They also indicated that regular evaluation should take place during the acting stage.

In recent years, however, implementations used varied methods for different objects; as Gasevic et al. (2016) explained, there are three most important themes in LA implementation – that is, the development of the predictor and indicators for a number of elements such as self-controlled learning skills, student engagement and academic performance; the visualization to search and construe data and to prompt corrective measures; and finally the beginning of interventions to outline the learning environment. Well, this always poses a test for education establishments, leading to common voices of "How do we start the process for the adoption of institutional LA?", "How do we implement the LA process successfully?" and "To what extent can the process of LA improve the QA in this case?"

Thus, the challenge of comprehending how theory and analytics are related is to shift "from clicks to constructs" in a just way (Knight & Buckingham Shum, 2013). According to Knight and Buckingham Shum (2013), "LA are a specific incarnation of the bigger shift to an algorithmically pervaded society, and their wider impact on education needs careful consideration" (p. 17). Knight, Buckingham Shum and Littleton (2014) have set forward a triadic interpretation of the connection among components of practice and theory in the progression of LA procedures (Knight et al., 2014). The Epistemology–Pedagogy–Assessment (EPA) Triad (Knight et al., 2014, p. 25) illustrates the inter-relations between the more or less theoretically based standpoint that goes through our pedagogical and assessment routines and guidelines and their fundamental epistemological insinuations and expectations.

LA as an innovative learning tool has the possibility to back up the existing educational practices. In the EPA Triad, the theoretical and useful drivers for which such empirical are formulated are firstly assessment and pedagogy, which are formed on the basis of a hierarchical structure, and secondly, they are all taken into configuration in a Venn graph form with a better overlay denoting a bigger complimentary of the theoretical standpoint (Knight et al., 2014). For example, LA has the potential to marginalize students who are weak in critical-thinking skills so that alternative ways of engaging activities should be introduced. This fundamentally then deploys a given LA tool to prompt a pledge to a specific educational worldview intended to develop a certain type of learner (i.e., personalized learning).

Knight et al. (2014) provided a set of six "W" questions to ponder before advancing using LA: First, "What are we measuring?" which alarms the basis of constructs on what is considered "knowledge" in relation to the facts and skills we need our students to acquire for "students to come to know" (e.g., the ability to apply theory of leadership into workplace). Second, "How are we measuring?" which relates to questions regarding ways in which analytic methods imply particular epistemology, putting the reliability of assessment methods aside (Knight et al., 2014). Third, "Why is this knowledge important to us?" for which the answer may somewhat be relevant to the type of learning theory that the analytics lays inside and to find out the instrumental goals on the topic of the analytics contribution to particular skills, such as employability skills, connected to pedagogical goals to care for a specific set of students for instance (Knight et al., 2014). Fourth, "Who is the analytic for?" which regards the needs for the analytics discernments at various stages of a system and the capability of individual analytic approaches such as dashboards to support students in developing learning, educators in developing their own capacity to use and administrators' understanding on the development's cohort and uses (Knight et al., 2014). Certainly ethical implications arise in the use of student data. Lastly, "Where does the assessment happen?" which concerns where LA is happening in reaction to the task and where LA can add value to meaningful learning experiences for students. It also depends on the particular learning system, as different systems shape the data obtained, which is always the practical concern regarding the validity and reliability of methods rather than the related epistemology concerns (Knight et al., 2014).

The EPA Triad depicts the connections among fundamentals of theory and practice in the progression of LA as a tool to improvise student learning. Tools can be utilized in multiple ways and must not be secluded from the context of usage, as concluded by Knight and Buckingham (2013). Whether bearing in mind one presently using LA, how one may perform in the future or undeniably when planning new tools for a fresh context, guidance and reflection on EPA in deploying LA within a given context are basic.

1.3 What Baffles Us?

New demands and opportunities today have placed unprecedented pressure on people's capacity to deal with uncertainty and adapt to changes, whether due to higher accountability as an educationalist or concerns regarding affordability. This encompasses students' learning processes and outcomes, including their acquired skills, competencies or knowledge, thereby placing pressure on universities at all levels. A few years back, technology-driven improvement was instigated to alter higher education, introducing fresh methods in learning and teaching to address the needs of the 21st century and hence increasing employability to combat the issue of graduates not able to secure suitable jobs (DeMillo, 2017). Besides, there are several concerns in students' learning processes and outcomes today, including incompletion of programs, integration of formal and informal learning approaches, knowledge management, 21st-century skills, transfer of knowledge, new methods of teaching and curriculum, quality of teaching, capacity of teachers for learning reform, and technology infrastructure and ethical use of data (Zilvinskis et al., 2017; DeMillo, 2017; Elmes, 2017; Bates, 2015; Granados, 2015; Gasevic et al., 2016; West et al., 2018; Henard & Roseveare, 2012; Zhou, 2018; Ferguson & Clow, 2017).

There are multiple definitions of LA, but the industry-preferred one that comes from the International Conference on Learning Analytics (LAK, 2011) is "Learning Analytics is the measurement, collection, analytics and reporting of data about learners and their content, for the purposes of understanding and optimizing learning and the environment in which it occurs" (p. 1). Effective use of data via LA is thus a critical component of a digital learning strategy to personalize instruction for a greater number of students, particularly to increase students' achievement at the tertiary level.

Thille and Zimmaro (2017) wrote that LA incorporates online learning initiatives (OLI) to establish a model utilizing educational technology aimed at changing the affiliation of technology practice, research and learning to improve learning outcomes, including the interpretation of learning process data to predict success. In addition, Buyarski et al. (2017) stated that LA efforts are profoundly restructuring how HEIs evaluate student achievement by focusing on students' learning outcomes and retention to accomplish the complete goal. Can the completion of goal be achieved from the perspective of higher education in Malaysia? Pistilli and Arnold (2010) also asserted that LA's prediction model looks at pre-entry attributes to evaluate risks, helping needy students reduce risks for course failure and incompletion of program, which in turn reduces burden of cost of education. Clow (2012) emphasized that learners benefit from personalized information in the LA cycle. Wong (2017) emphasized the benefits of LA for stakeholders, which includes the reduction of student attrition rate by monitoring students' learning processes to facilitate early identification of risk, leading to higher achievement rate and lower dropout rate; achievement of cost-effectiveness to the management through the integration of LA with the LMS, for instance; resource optimization and enhancement of effective communication through real-time feedback; and better evaluation of pedagogies and instructional design for quality improvement and assurance. However, according to Ferguson and Clow (2017), LA has not yet fully redeemed its promises. Macfadyen et al. (2014) highlight the significant challenges in implementing cultural, infrastructural, technological, and organizational changes to teaching practices, emphasizing the crucial role of LA in policy formulation.

According to the aforementioned mentioned studies, despite the point that LA is relatively new in research and professional practices in higher education today, especially in Malaysia, QA is frequently omitted from studies pertaining to the broader field of LA. In different investigative contexts that address concerns in the literature review study for the Malaysian and international scenarios, researchers aim to find out to what extent LA can be a tool to improvise students' learning processes and learning outcomes for QA, despite barriers such as strategic direction, human adaptability to cultural change, technological and infrastructural support, teaching and learning policies and management, as well as the ethical use of data (West et al., 2018). As put forward by Scalter (2017) and Rick (2013), issues of job redundancy, additional workload and time management as factors affecting the level of comfort and willingness to accept changes to current practices relating to job roles and possible causes for people to repel transformation, such as the alignment of trust and beliefs of staff, have critical implications for "job", cautioning educators to be mindful of the unintended consequences.

In response to the aforementioned, the academic quality system in Malaysia has also progressed and enriched into an affirmative path (Mokhtar et al., 2014). Having said that, QA on the other hand is a rounded method covering every procedure in HEIs to assist students and other stakeholders in achieving anticipated quality values (Kahveci et al., 2012). In view of the various pertinent concerns and challenges that necessitate to be looked into to safeguard quality of the programs, the development of Academic Quality Assurance (AQA) in HEIs has been deliberated repeatedly amid upper management of HEIs. In Malaysia, an agency that is accountable for the AQA is the Malaysian Qualifications Agency (MQA), which has been in operation since 2007 and has established a qualification outline or framework called the Malaysian Qualifications Framework (MQF). Over time, the subsequent implementation of two important documents plays a vital role – they are codes of practice for program accreditation (COPPA) and codes of practice for institutional audit (COPIA). Program accreditation is a procedure that ensures that the programs and institutions achieve the applicable standards of quality and veracity set by MQA and in compliance with MQF.

Various issues in AQA were highlighted in the recent years by both accountable bodies/agencies and scholars (Mokhtar et al., 2014). According to Grapragasem et al. (2014), there are four existing trends in Malaysian higher education, namely knowledge-based society, governance, teaching and learning, and globalization. In relation to this, Grapragasem et al. (2014) also emphasized that the important components that affect the quality of education are QA, academic employability and English-language proficiency, though employability has been deliberated and used as a dimension of education quality in HEIs. In other words, problems that need to be emphasized are monitoring AQA by means of effective measurement and data-based linkages, improving AQA through a structured design of continuous quality improvement (CQI) and collaboration throughout the HEIs.

According to Dix and Leavesley (2015), LA offers apparent advantages to high-ranking administration in a progressively metrics-compelled realm of higher education and unswervingly supports student learning; hence, it should be used by academics. The success of QA is thus dependent on the support of the academics, as QA can be achieved through the implementation of LA in the programs. Hence, in conclusion, the nature of worldwide culture and economic equilibriums has shifted as we have entered the 21st century. These shifts and changes are reflected in some of the issues and challenges facing higher education and also in learning and teaching. It disrupts not only traditional classroom teaching and learning methods but also the value-added recital of information by technology. Affordable quality is the goal that allows students to pay only for the value they received, which in fact will be the dramatic shift in the landscape of education. That is where the area of current issues in student learning processes and outcomes will be explored, and AQA is to ensure that changes can be made through the application of LA in HEIs.

Studies will be guided based on the domain of the student learning processes and learning outcomes, adhering to a successful empirically validated theory that demonstrated in other countries.

Nonetheless, LA is a new technology in the education environment in Malaysia (West et al., 2018). Most importantly, not many studies have been conducted in relation to the drivers of LA to QA in HEI in Malaysia, despite there being evidence that the LA model used internationally has shown significant contributions in academics, as anticipated in terms of meeting students' learning needs. As the imperfect world is advancing relentlessly toward an uncertain future, gaps are becoming increasingly pronounced; hence, researchers have to explore the benefits of LA, what are the learning issues in the context of study where LA impacts the management and faculty in students' learning processes and outcomes in higher education in Malaysia, the issues and challenges associated with the implementation of LA toward achieving QA, and the implications of the LA transformation process on employment within higher education. Consequently, researchers should explore how we can redirect this initiative toward sustainability, especially considering that change is impossible without LA.

Hence, two elements have inspired this study. First, assuming the mounting prominence of LA in students' learning processes and learning outcomes, it remains imperative for HEIs in Malaysia to comprehend the contribution of LA towards impacting students' learning processes and outcomes. Second, the research also illustrates that by applying LA, QA of higher education could also capitulate an enhanced benchmark height. It is therefore important to investigate LA as a process of ongoing contribution to students' learning processes and learning outcomes towards achieving QA of education in Malaysia; after all, this implementation for achieving QA is a journey.

References

1st International Conference on Learning Analytics and Knowledge 2011. (2010). http://web.archive.org/web/20101220223648/ http://tekri.athabascau.ca/analytic

Arroway, P., Morgan, G., O'Keefe, M., & Yanosky, R. (2016). Learning analytics in higher education. *EDUCAUSE*. http://library.educause.edu/~/media/files/library/2016/2/ers15041a.pdf

Baker, B. M. (2007). *A conceptual framework for making knowledge actionable through capital formation* [Doctoral dissertation, University of Maryland University College. University Press].

Bates, A. W. (2015). Teaching in a digital age – guidelines for designing teaching and learning. *Creative commons attribution-non-commercial 4.0 international license*. https://bccampus.ca/open-textbook-project/

Buyarski, C., Murray, J., & Torstrick, R. (2017). Learning analytics across a statewide system. In J. Zilvinskis & V. Boarder (Eds.), *Learning analytics in higher education. New directions for higher education, 179* (Fall). Jossey-Bass.

Campbell, J. P., DeBlois, P. B., & Oblinger, D. G. (2007). Academic analytics: A new tool for a new era. *EDUCASE Review*, *42*(4).

Chinomona, R. (2013). *Elements of quality assurance at institutions of higher education: Vaal University of Technology in South Africa*. https://doi.org/10.5910/mjss.2013.v4n14p643. https://www.researchgate.net/publication/257928331_Elements_of_Quality_Assurance_at_Institutions_of_Higher_Education_Vaal_University_of_Technology_in_South_Africa

Clow, D. (2012). The learning analytics cycle: Closing the loop. In D. Gasevic & S. Buckingham Shum (Eds.), *Proceedings from the 2nd international learning analytics and knowledge conference* (p. 1340138). ACM. http://doi.org/10.1145/2330601.2330636

DeMillo, R. A. (2017). *Revolution in higher education – how a small band of innovators will make college accessible and affordable*. MIT Press.

Dix, A., & Leavesley, J. (2015). *Learning analytics for the academics: An Action perspective*. http://alandix.com/academic/papers/JUCS-action-analytics-2015/jucs_action_analytics-2015.pdf

Dron, J., & Anderson, T. (2011). Three generations of distance learning education pedagogy. *The International Review of Research in Open and Distribution Learning*, *12*(3). http://www.irrodl.org/index.php/irrodl/article/view/890/1663

Dziuban, C., Moskal, P., Cavanagh, T., & Watts, A. (2012). Analytics that inform the university: Using data you already have. *Journal of Asynchronous Learning Network*, *16*(3), 21–38.

Elias, T. (2011). *Learning analytics: Definitions, processes, and potential*. http://learningalaytics.net/LearningAnalyticsDfinitionsPRocessesPotential.pdf

Elmes, J. (2017). *Six significant challenges for technology in higher education in 2017*. https://www.timeshighereducation.com/features/six-significant-challenges-technology-higher-education-2017

Fahd, K., & Miah, S. J. M. (2023). Designing and evaluating a big data analytics approach for predicting students' success factors. *Journal of Big Data*, *10*(1), 159.

Ferguson, R., & Clow, D. (2017). Learning analytics: Avoiding failure. *EDUCAUSE Review*. https://er.educause.edu/articles/2017/7/learning-analytics-avoiding-failure

Freeman, S., O'Connor, E., Parks, J. W., Cunningham, M., Hurley, D. H., Haak, D., ... Wenderoth, M. P. (2007). Prescribed active learning increases performance in introductory biology. *CBE-Life Science Education*, *6*(2), 132–139. https://doi.org/10.1187/cbe.06-09-0194

Gasevic, D., Dawson, S., & Pardo, A. (2016). How do we start? State and directions of learning analytics adoption. *International council for open and distance education*. http://icde.memberclicks.net/assets/RESOURCES/dragan la report%20cc%20licence.pdf

Granados, J. (2015). *The challenges of higher education in the 21st century*. http://www.guninetwork.org/articles/challenges-higher-education-21st-century

Grapragasem, S., Krishnan, A., & Mansor, A. N. (2014). Current trends in Malaysia higher education and the effect on education policy and practice: An overview. *International Journal of Higher Education*, *3*, 85. https://doi.org/10.5430/ijhe.v3n1p85

Henard, F., & Roseveare, D. (2012). *Fostering quality teaching in higher education: Policies and practices*. http://www.oecd.org/education/imhe/QT%20policies%20and%20practices.pdf

Kahveci, T. C., Uygun, O., Yurtsever, U., & Ilyas, S. (2012). Quality assurance in higher education institutions using strategic information system. International conference on New Horizons in education INTE2012. Elseview Ltd. *Social and Behavioral Sciences*, *55*(2012), 161–167. https://ac.els-cdn.com/S1877042812039523/1-s2.0-S1877042812039523-main.pdf?_tid=f60097fe-84e6-43df-b5eb-afba57505d2d&acdnat=1540069099_febdc92d631544ed80ab7da7ac6ba3d5

Knight, S., & Shum, S. B. (2013). Chapter 1: Theory and learning analytics. In *Handbook of learning analytics*. Connected Intelligence Center. University of Technology Sydney. https://doi.org/10.18608/hla17.001

Knight, S., Shum, S. B., & Littleton, K. (2014). Epistemology, assessment, pedagogy: Where learning meets analytics in the middle space. *Journal of Learning Analytics*, *1*(2). http://epress.lib.uts.edu.au/journals/index.php/JLA/article/view/3538

Lonn, S., McKay, T. A., & Teasley, S. D. (2017). Cultivating institutional capacities for learning analytics. In J. Zilvinskis & V. Boarder (Eds.), *Learning analytics in higher education. New directions for higher education, 179* (Fall). Jossey-Bass.

Macfadyen, L. P., Awson, S., Pardo, A., & Gasevic, D. (2014). Embracing big data in complex educational system: The learning analytics imperative and policy challenge. *Research & Practice in Assessment*, *9*(Winter), 17–28. http://www.rpajournal.com/dev/wp-content/uploads/2014/10/A2.pdf

Mokhtar, R., Rahman, A. A., Othman, S. H., & Ali, N. (2014). Malaysian academic quality assurance system in the context of issues, challenges and best practices. Knowledge management international conference (KMICe). *Research Gate Malaysia*, 12–15. https://www.researchgate.net/publication/267633436_Malaysian_Academic_Quality_AssuranceSystem_in_the_context_of_issues_challenges_and_best_practices?_esc=publicationCoverPdf&el=1_x_3&enrichId=rgreq-691dccb67fac0146c7a8eb08a4ddb8fe-XXX&enrichSource=Y292ZXJQYWdlOzI2NzYzMzQzNjtBUzoxNTg4ODc3MDEzOTM0MDhAMTQxNDg5MzE4ODY0OA%3D%3D

OECD. (2017, April 15). *21st century skills: Learning for the digital age*. https://www.oecd-forum.org/users/50593-oecd/posts/20442-21st-century-skills-learning-for-the-digital-age

Pardo, A. (2014). Designing learning analytics experience. In J. A. Larusson & B. White (Eds.), *Learning analytics: From research to practice* (pp. 15–38). Springer.

Picciano, A. G. (2012). The evolution of big data and learning analytics in America higher education. *Journal of Asynchronous Learning Networks*, *16*(3), 9–20. https://files.eric.ed.gov/fulltext/EJ982669.pdf

Pistilli, M. D., & Arnold, K. E. (2010). Purdue signals: Mining real-time academic data to enhance student success. *About Campus*, *15*(3), 22–24. Thousand Oaks California.

Reyes, J. A. (2015). The skinny on big data in education: Learning analytics simplified. *Tech Trends*, *59*(2), 75–79. https://eric.ed.gov/?id=EJ1050812

Rick, T. (2013). *Resistant to change is a problem*. https://www.torbenrick.eu/blog/change-management/change-is-not-the-problem-resistance-to-change-is-the-problem/

Scalter, N. (2017). Learning analytics adoption and implementation plan. *Jisc Effective Learning Analytic*. https://analytics.jiscinvolve.org/wp/2017/03/21/learning-analytics-adoption-and-implementation-trends

Sclater, N., Peasgood, A., & Mullan, J. (2016). *Learning analytics in higher education – A review of UK and international practice full report*. https://www.jisc.ac.uk/sites/default/files/learning-analytics-in-he-v2_0.pdf

Siemens, G., & Baker, R. (2012). Learning analytics and educational data mining: Towards communication and collaboration. *Proceedings of the 2nd international conference on learning analytics and knowledge*. http://www.columbia,edu/~rsb2162/LAKs%20reformatting%20v2.pdf

Tasir, Z., Kew, S. N., West, Z., Abdullah, Z., & Toohey, D. (2016). Collaborative research between Malaysian and Australian universities on learning analytics: Challenges and strategies. *International Journal of Educational and Pedagogical Sciences*, *10*(8), 2900–2906. https://waset.org/publications/10005255/collaborative-research-between-malaysian-and-australian-universities-on-learning-analytics-challenges-and-strategies

Thille, C., & Zimmaro, D. (2017). Incorporating learning analytics in the classroom. In J. Zilvinskis & V. Boarder (Eds.), *Learning analytics in higher education. New directions for higher education, 179* (Fall). Jossey-Bass.

West, D., Luzeckyj, A., Tasir, Z., & Toohey, D. P. (2018). Learning analytics experience among academics in Australia and Malaysia: A comparison. *Australian Journal of Educational Technology*, *34*(3), 122–139. https://doi.org/10.14742ajet.3836

Wong, T. M. B. (2017). Learning analytics in higher education: Analysis in case studies. *Asia Association of Open Universities Journal*, *12*(1), 21–40. https://doi.org/10.1108/AAOUJ-01-2017-0009

Wright, M. C., McKay, T., Hershock, C., Miller, K., & Tritz, J. (2014). Better than expected: Using learning analytics to promote student success in gateway science. *Change: The Magazine of Higher Learning*, *46*(1), 28–34. https://doi.org/10.1080/00091383.2014.867209

Zhou, X. F. (2018). The UQ experience as an analytics driven university. *Panel presentation on "The analytics organization: Challenges and directions" of HELP university annual convocation 21st strategy seminar 2018*. Kuala Lumpur, Malaysia.

Zilvinskis, J., & Boarder, V. (2017). *Learning analytics in higher education. New directions for higher education, 179* (Fall). Jossey-Bass.

2 Pertinent Theories and Concepts for AI-Powered Education

2.1 Introduction

Whether we agree or we don't, it is a fact that learners from as far back as 40 years ago completed required studies and started work that can often last for a lifetime (Siemens, 2004). During those days, knowledge was measured in decades; however, it has grown exponentially, where currently in many fields, knowledge is measured in months. Discussions have been made on the significant trends in learning thus far, wherein students are anticipated to adopt various technology-based gears and participate in online discussions, presenting assignments with active learning approaches like problem-based learning or projects where educators are acting more as facilitators these days, especially keeping pace with the needs of 21st-century learners. In addition, AI also provides opportunities for personalizing learning experiences based on individual student data and learning styles, which can be connected to learning theories and AI-powered platforms in adaptive learning. In other words, students have to be entrepreneurial and employment-savvy. How have the learning theories been developed to establish a pedagogical framework for LA that maximizes students' learning? Considering how LA is measured based on knowledge, pedagogies and assessment (Knight et al., 2014), students' learning processes is reflected in the review of LA and its benefits, while students' learning outcomes are predominantly reflected in the review of QA. Hence, all aspects in relation to the specific issues concerned were investigated, focusing on LA in the context QA in higher education in Malaysia from a global perspective.

2.2 LA and Its Relevance to Education Theory/ Learning Theories

LA is a tool for educators and learners. Researchers are still trying to secure a robust measure of learning in the application of "big data" approaches. Experiencing a deep structural shift toward an algorithmically pervaded society, together with its wider educational benefits impacting students, necessitates an exploration of learning theories and education theories to reflect how LA is connected with each other.

DOI: 10.4324/9781003584520-2

Empirically, education theory is an umbrella term for many theories that explain the applications, integration and purpose of learning and education. All those theories shall construct and explain how we best learn so that lecturers can correspondingly apply research findings to practice. From Pavlov's classical conditioning theories, which are mostly behavioral, till today, as the field has evolved toward the 21st century, learning theories began to splinter off into discovery learning by Piaget, as well as the study of social cognition theory by Bandera (Siemens, 2004). These include behaviorist learning, cognitive learning, constructionist learning and connectivism theory, which also guide the research framework to be conceptualized accordingly.

In education, constructivism, cognitivism and behaviorism are the three broad learning and teaching theories mostly used in the design of learning and teaching environment (Siemens, 2004). Over the last two decades, technology has reorganized how we go about living day to day, how we connect and how we learn and re-learn. In that sense, learning ideologies and learning procedures that were grounded have been extended through learning theories based on different learning needs over time in different contexts in the underlying social environment. It is thus a way of being in the lens of emotion and skills brought about as a result of experiences and interactions with other people, as defined by Driscoll (2000), cited in Siemens (2004). Philosophically, constructivism, cognitivism and behaviorism are building on epistemological tradition, looking at how people learn. These learning theories hold on the impression that knowledge is attainable through experience, reasoning or thinking. However, our aptitude to learn what we want for tomorrow is more significant than what we discern today. What is vital is not so much about how much you know but about how to stimulate known knowledge at the point of utilization and meet the requirements at that point in time.

As stated by Siemens (2004), as knowledge advances to develop and progress, the right to use what is required is more imperative than what the learner presently retains. "Connectivism" thus offers a design of learning that recognizes and acknowledges the tectonic changes in society where learning is no longer an inner, personal action (Siemens, 2004). Therefore, "Connectivism" yields discernment into learning skills and tasks required for learners to thrive in a digital epoch which in turn creates a huge impact on the learning experience of students. While behaviorism is the theory that aids us in examining how people comprehend and how people adapt to reset standards, cognitivism is the theory that examines how learning happens through psychological connotations; constructivism is the theory that examines the significance of human action as an acute purpose of acquiring knowledge; and connectivism comprises technology and establishing link as learning actions into digital era. Factual proof from educational robotics utilizations, grounded in learning theories, advocates that a few literature suggestions can be beneficial in practice such as project-based theories and experiential theories, omitting an enhancement in students' enthusiasm and hands-on activities (Behrens et al.,

2010; Campbell, 2002; Hall et al., 2008; Hoffmann et al., 2015; Jou et al., 2010; Kurkovsku, 2014).

Having to reflect on educational theory again, Confucius and Aristotle were early few theorists who advocated learning by actually performing it; Socrates demonstrated how to learn by asking questions, probing and critical thinking – all approaches that remain very pertinent in today's problem-based learning classrooms (Boss, 2011). When we move to the 20th-century American educational theorist and philosopher John Dewey, he considers that learning based on experience is compelled by student attentiveness. Dewey even defied the customary interpretation of the student as an unreceptive receiver of knowledge, where he disputed that an alternative for vigorous experiences is the one that develops students for continuous learning about a vibrant world (Boss, 2011; Williams, 2017). Jean Piaget, a Swiss developmental psychologist, assisted us to comprehend how we create sense from our experiences at diverse ages (Boss, 2011). His discernments positioned the groundwork for the constructivist method of education, wherein students build on what they distinguish by probing questions, scrutinizing, interrelating with others and echoing on these experiences. So, acknowledging real-life learning, which is messy and complex, is thus an effective learning method preparing learners for lifelong learning.

Academics implicitly trust and have faith that higher education supports knowledge and learning; it provides access to get a decent employment so that we are able to lead a significant life. Living in a world in crisis where time is fluid, things do not last. Is that true? Academics are faced with issues and challenges, especially in students' learning processes and outcomes, particularly across time and contexts. What are those issues in learning? Besides, instructional design is an emergent area given the expanse of online programs we are currently experiencing; it is becoming progressively more essential that we generate learning experiences that "work", and this is becoming more challenging year after year as courses strive for learners' attention (Ferriman, 2017). Instructional designers are entrusted with identifying the finest manner to impart fresh data to a target audience. Forget about the notion of the "one size fits all" approach (Ferriman, 2017). Any instructional designer valuing their worth is going to want to noticeably establish distinctive objectives from the perspective of those who will be participating in the course. Once these are eliminated, the technique of imparting the content can be carefully chosen. Among learning theories, cognitivism emphasizes prior knowledge and cognitive processes that can be modeled by AI to predict academic performance. Similarly, constructivism focuses on how students build knowledge, and AI can analyze learning activities to predict how effectively students are constructing understanding. Haron et al. (2025) investigated data mining strategies by evaluating three classification algorithms: RepTree, k-NN and Naïve Bayes. RepTree achieved the highest percentage in terms of accuracy (i.e., 94.38%), which means it is the most suitable model for predicting student performance. This system provides insights on academic performance and resource allocation to multiple stakeholders, such as students, parents and educators. Hence, those issues mentioned are addressed around the notion of theories conceptually. In this case, theoretical framework is structured based on LA and its benefits, quality concepts and QA, and stakeholder theory. Chapter 3 provides a comprehensive critical assessment of learning theories that complement LA, guiding students' learning experiences for optimal benefit through respective methodologies.

2.2.1 Behaviorist Learning Theory

It is a philosophy of learning established on the notion that our behaviors are learned through habituation (Cherry, 2018), wherein environmental factors influence our responses and our reactions to surrounding inducements form our actions. According to this school of thought by behaviorist B.F. Skinner, behavior can be examined in an orderly and discernable way regardless of inner and psychological conditions, like reasoning, feelings and temperaments (Cherry, 2018). How? Behaviorist methods have long been engaged in education to encourage learning through reinforcement, consequences and other practical classroom applications. It is about when one learns by creating a connotation for a particular conduct and the results of the conduct. For instance, ramifications occur instantaneously following an action. Ramifications might be emotional/interpersonal or even unconscious, immediate or continuing, extrinsic or intrinsic, expected or unexpected, material or symbolic (a failing grade), positive or negative (Zhou & Brown, 2015).

Discussions on transformation of learning methods to meet the learning needs for future skills and related topics are at the top of the list for tertiary education today. Practices expected based on the relevant theories may no longer elicit approval from lecturers for satisfactory performance. For example, Robert Gagne (1985), cited in Ullah et al. (2015), proposed the nine events of instruction, emphasizing the individuality of learners in the instructional process to improve teaching. The structure consists of a sequence of actions built on the behaviorist approach to gaining knowledge.

These actions follow an organized instructional design procedure, generating a supple model where actions can be adjusted to tailor to diverse learning conditions. Truthfully, it is one of the desired instructional strategy models, as it offers a thorough arrangement for creating effective eLearning, higher teacher's performance and better understanding of students with higher retention of knowledge (Ullah et al., 2015). The nine stages are as follows: to capture devotion of the learners through motivations that clasp and involve their common sense; to notify learners of the goals establishing the anticipated results and standards for evaluating accomplishments; to kindle memory of previous learning capitalizing current knowledge before presenting fresh knowledge and constructing on it; to give content delivering in straightforwardly in unpreserved portions; to give students directions, guiding them with illustrations, case studies and additional teaching backing to complement information; to stimulate their actions by engaging them through various actions, encompassing remembering, applying and evaluating knowledge; to offer response/feedback reinforcing knowledge with instantaneous response, especially remedial feedback; to evaluate their performance testing their knowledge with proven translucent standards; and to improve retention and transmission to employment using content retention approaches (job aids, summarizing, concept maps, rephrasing, etc.).

The evolution of this theory, grounded in the epistemological tradition of learning, is thus significant in the current digital age, simply equipping students with diverse learning experiences to prepare them for 21st-century survival skills (Zhou & Brown, 2015). This is simply because students expect much more beyond that. For achieving the best learning outcomes in HEIs today, implementing techniques such as attaining a score of 80% or greater for the final assessment to be deemed non-compulsory is practical and effective. Either completing all coursework on time, even if the lowest grade is disregarded, or maintaining perfect attendance will earn a 'homework pass'. Abdul Jalil et al. (2021) in their study found that students' expectation for using LA in higher education is for self-assessment, planning of study and receiving personalized recommendations.

The reinforcement learning approach, influenced by behaviorist psychology, involves a computational method in education where computers or machines learn to optimize responses based on a numerical collective reward signal (Sutton & Barto, 2017). In instances where the student is not informed on which actions to acquire, they should, as an alternative, ascertain which activities produce the most incentive by venturing into them. This concept can be further examined in the realm of computer learning, particularly within the framework of Markov Decision Processes (MDP), where numerous reinforcement learning algorithms employ dynamic software design systems to optimize learner outcomes. Reinforcement learning is different from regular monitored learning in that precise input/output sets are not given and sub-optimal activities need not be clearly rectified. Rather the emphasis is on performance, which encompasses looking for an equilibrium amid discovering (of unexplored territory) and taking advantage (of present knowledge). However, further empirical research and practical implementation are needed to prove the effectiveness of LA grounded on the theory of reinforcement learning, irrespective of its capacity to facilitate the attainment of students' learning outcomes within the standards, quality and relevance of the academic QA system, contingent upon its foundation in the theory/model of LA across various domains of knowledge.

2.2.2 Cognitive Learning Theory

Zhou and Brown (2015) cited on Piaget's work explains the basis where constructionist theories are built, positing that knowledge is made and learning happens when learners make goods or artifacts that are individually pertinent and important. In addition, Piaget believes that intelligence growth is a lifetime practice, but that is when prescribed active thoughts are reached and no new configurations are needed. The intellectual development of adults involves the acquisition of complex strategies through the accumulation of knowledge. A vital repercussion of Piaget's theory is tailoring the instruction to the students' developmental stage. The teaching content must align with the developmental stage of the student.

The instructor's task is to assist learning by providing a diversity of involvements and experiences. Moreover, the teacher is a facilitator who assists in comprehending the overwhelming amount of information available to students (Zhou & Brown, 2015). At this end, "discovery learning" offers chances for students to discover and investigate, and in so doing inspires fresh and new comprehension. There are chances that permit learners of diverse mental intensities to team work every so often, inspiring younger learners to excel to more matured understandings. Yet another suggestion for teaching is the utilization of substantial "hands-on" feats/experiences to aid learners to study. In other words, data can guide instructors on how to personalize learning of individual students so as to achieve the different components of QA in terms of its quality and standards.

Cognitivism theories in education are extensively used that are based on learning aims found in Bloom's taxonomies as cited in Bates (2015). In 1956, Benjamin Bloom formed an arrangement structure of quantifiable verbs to define and bring together diverse cognitive learning levels (Gutierrez, 2015). In 2001, the six scopes were revised by Anderson and Krathwohi and are identified as the "Revised Taxonomy", which emphasizes advancing students beyond the foundational levels of knowledge and recall into deeper understanding, critical thinking and the application of knowledge to enhance their unique problem-solving skills. It is an excellent means for forming learning goals that involve students with the content and instilling new conceptions and knowledge. Deep learning or active learning as described in this theory is in line with the trends in real-time learning, such as LA, which provides a useful structure for instructors to engage in interactive discussions with students on the design, delivery and evaluation of lessons and assignments more effectively.

In practicing this, this notion of brain as machine has steered a number of technology-grounded advances in instruction, including intellectual systems founded on dividing learning into a sequence of practicable pace and directing the most appropriate next step based on learner's responses. According to Bates (2015), and with reference to the previous chapter, adaptive learning is the latest addition to such development. Others also include predetermined learning outcomes, as noted by Bates (2015), which are based on the study and growth of diverse types of perceptive actions such as understanding and assessment. Problem-based learning, grounded in analytical thinking processes and instructional design methodologies, aims to address instructional design while assuring successful learning outcomes. Omar et al.

(2024a) suggest a framework using AI to personalize professional development (PD) training. Learner data can be used to design training content as well as delivery and assessment techniques that suit individual needs. This also promotes the culture of continuous learning and improves skill acquisition. In addition, Omar et al. (2024b) also recommend a framework for integrating AI into postgraduate teaching for professionals. The framework is based on a systematic literature evaluation aimed at utilizing AI to promote active engagement and learning exchanges among professional learners.

2.2.3 Constructivist Learning Theory

Constructivist places emphasis on the significance of free will awareness and community influence on learning, as cited in (Bates, 2015). Constructionism supports a learner-centered approach, emphasizing learning to discover, wherein learners utilize pre-existing knowledge to acquire more, inherently subjective insights (Bates, 2015). Learners study while participating in project-centered learning where they create links among diverse thoughts and parts of knowledge assisted by the instructor by drilling instead of employing teachers or guiding step-by-step. The key point raised by Bates (2015) is that, for constructivists, learning is perceived as fundamentally a process of social nature, necessitating communication among students, teachers and others. In other words, this social practice may not be efficiently substituted by technology, even though technology might assist it. LA and AI can help in providing personalized insights, feedback and recommendations based on individual student interactions and performance data. Dahri et al. (2024) stated that AI tools can provide more flexible academic support anytime or at any place. This study explores factors that influence students' usage of AI tools in Pakistan and Malaysia. The research found that students who used AI tools for academic improvement have higher tendency to be satisfied and view positive impacts on their learning.

Against this theoretical background, problem-centered learning has been practiced as a concrete instructional approach in economics, medicine, engineering and other domains for more than 50 years. In this methodology, learners are confronted to resolve glitches or create mockups that stimulate actual life (Bates, 2015). Even though glitches are explained beforehand by the teacher, they have a tendency to be intricate and even chaotic and cannot be unraveled by only one right answer. Unlike textbook-compelled teaching, the learner is in charge of probing and determining responses in problem-centered learning. Learners utilize technology tools, as all experts do, to connect, work together, carry out research, investigate, produce and publish their writings for genuine readers. As an alternative to preparing reports for books, for instance, students could undertake a literature project in which they produce audio book reviews, put them on a blog and solicit criticism from classmates in comparable classes from different states or nations. Indeed, Driscoll stated, as cited by Simmens (2004), that constructivists suggest that learners understand their experience by creating knowledge, and they frequently choose and follow their personal learning. Constructivist too concede that real-life learning is chaotic and intricate. Hence, classrooms, which imitate the "fuzziness" of their education, will be more efficient in getting students ready for learning throughout lifetime (Simmens, 2004).

Several inclinations have steered the embracing of project-centered learning as an education strategy for the 21st century. Cognitive experts have enhanced our grasp of how people learn, how people cultivate expertise and how people initiate reasoning at a greater level (Bates, 2015). Areas stretching from neuroscience to social psychology have contributed to our understanding of what conditions create the best environment for learning. Culture, context and the social nature of learning all have a role in shaping the learner's experience. Although problem-centered learning is applicable throughout different subject matters, it constantly accentuates dynamic, student-focused learning. What makes this strategy more likely to enhance comprehension compared to memorization? The key role is applicability (Bates, 2015). Current learners are facing multifaceted tests when they are done with formal education. The ability to resolve complications, work together and think creatively are becoming indispensable skills not only for finding employment in the future but also for dealing with challenging matters in the domestic and global communities. Arvinth (2024) did a study on the use of AI in Indian higher education. He found that AI tools such as platforms for personalized learning and chatbots were commonly used, and most of the respondents felt that the tools improved their grades. However, there have been concerns on data privacy and bias, necessitating tactful implementation.

According to David (2015), Bandura's Social Learning Theory suggests that individuals learn from one another via modeling, observation and imitation. The theory by Albert Bandura, proposed in 1925, is often regarded as a link between behaviorist and cognitive learning philosophies, as it incorporates attention, memory and motivation in the process of learning through the observation of others' behaviors, attitudes and the consequences of those actions. Social learning theory describes human actions in terms of continuous equal interface between behavioral, cognitive and ecological stimuli. According to Ferguson (2012), social LA thus develops new tools for teachers and students drawing on experience from the learning sciences; it redefines the learning landscape by building on theories of effective learning, wherein LA enhances the process, focusing on how learners form knowledge together in their cultural and community settings.

Social learning theory sets on a number of rudimentary suppositions about learning and behavior. For instance, one supposition deals with the opinion that environmental, behavioral and personal factors impact one another, meaning an individual's current responsibilities are a creation of constant communication between contextual, cognitive and behavioral factors (David, 2015). At the end of the day, learners must have faith that, if they finish learning responsibilities effectively, the results they attain are significant, beneficial or commendable of the determination essential to grasp them. Learners' learning is governed by their personal point of view and principles; thus, modules that focus on real-life applications and the significance of model content to learners' personal life are emphasized.

When project-focused learning is integrated with technology, it may be viewed as a 21st-century idea, although it is grounded on a well-established foundation (Boss, 2011). Projects propel the world forward. When the project method is active in the classroom, learners get chances to get involved in actual problem-solving too. Instead of learning about history from a textbook, learners turn into historians as they produce a film about an experience that altered their people. Indeed, projects give learners a real-world perspective for learning and create a resilient "need to know". Boss (2011) asserts that motivation is a crucial element of projects, providing students with choice and agency, hence customizing the learning experience. The blueprint indicates that projects are open-ended. This signifies learners must reflect and assess various resolutions and, perhaps, stand up for their selections. All these activities involve thinking skills in higher order. To be able to meet the trend of being digital savvy, it is adequate just to learn how to read. Current learners need to steer and assess a massive pile of data, requiring articulacy in technology together with the progression of critical thinking skills so that learners can not only comprehend this information but also enhance it with their personal influences (Boss, 2011). However, project-focused learning is always with its challenges. It's challenging for learners – and for instructors. Particularly for instructors who have never practiced this method before, projects call for preparation and managing skills that they might be unaccustomed to. Furthermore, it positions instructors as facilitators rather than experts in the classroom. Instructors will be at an advantage from professional growth to enhance their classroom "tool kit" of teaching approaches. Backing from managers, parents and other members of the community can assist instructors and learners to tackle challenges and make the best of the chances. As it achieves supporters and gains thrust, the education communal will carry on to give-and-take ideas and work together on projects, turning this prevailing technique of getting students ready for the future even better.

2.2.4 Connectivism Learning Theory

Another epistemological stance, connectivism, has surfaced recently that is mainly significant to a digital culture (Bates, 2015). In connectivism, it is the shared links among all the nodes in a linkage that have resulted in new domains of knowledge. Conferring to Simmens (2004), it is the links and how information transcends that result in knowledge, and how learning turns out to be a skill to get into substantial streams of information and to track those flows that are important. In the context of Siemens, Downes and Cormier, who created the earliest massive open online course (MOOC) in 2011 (Bates, 2015), the primary objective of an instructor appears to be the facilitation of an initial learning environment and perspective that fosters student collaboration while also aiding students in developing their personalized learning contexts that enable them to connect with a productive and successful network. Hamzah and Abu Seman (2024) conducted a study on existing QA frameworks with respect to online learning platforms. Results show their effectiveness depends on how education institutions implement those frameworks. Framework adaption needs to be accompanied with issues such as digital divide and student engagement so that students from the UK, Malaysia and the Middle East can acquire high-quality online learning experiences. Yang et al. (2024) also conducted another study where they proposed a big data mining approach for analyzing and predicting student performance in open and distance learning (ODL). The study examined factors such as academic structure and gender that create student profiles, which assist universities to identify students who are at risk and offer them focused support.

To ensure Outcome-Based Education (OBE) in the Malaysian code of practice for program certification/accreditation by MQA, the accuracy of instructional and learning methodologies must be implemented to meet the Program Learning Outcomes (PLO) and Course Learning Objectives (CLO) at HEIs (MQA, 2018a). To further enhance the validity of assessment, the assessment components at different levels are set in accordance with Bloom's six categories, namely remembering, understanding, applying, analyzing, evaluating and creating. Besides classroom delivery/attending lecturers, independent study with assigned reading text, self/team examination exercises, role play and case studies, as much as LA feedback and intervention, can be made effective – a popular medium used today is through MOOCs or other digital approaches in writing, individual research, online discussion and even small group collaboration (MQA, 2018a). Certainly, access to lecturers for consultation has to be formalized so as to fully facilitate students in digital platforms. All these are to ensure students do not just have rote learning of concepts but also engage in deeper learning and interpretation of those concepts. The matrix of CLO versus PLO as a whole can thus be an essential platform for LA's intervention to evaluate the effectiveness of QA procedures in relation to the extent to which programs meet the anticipated learning outcomes (MQA, 2018b).

According to Simmens (2004), our capability to study what we require for the future is more imperative than what we distinguish currently. The ability to access extensive resources to evaluate circumstances is a crucial talent. Also, connectivism acknowledges the monumental changes in culture, recognizing the impact of learning technologies and the ecological changes necessary for learners to flourish in the digital era (Simmens, 2004). As connectivism is still being developed and refined, it is presently extremely debatable, with lots of criticizers, especially in its approach to teaching and learning (Bates, 2015). Certainly, disapprovals may accumulate overtime as practices mend and new tools of valuation are established with increasing expertise. Most prominently, connectivism is the first theoretical effort to drastically reinspect the implications for learning using new communication technologies. Rahiman and Kodikal (2024) examined how AI revolutionizes education. AI personalizes learning and identifies students who are struggling in academics. However, successful implementation requires collaboration among diverse stakeholders, such as educators, students and technology providers. In addition, privacy concerns should be addressed by policymakers for supporting universities in developing infrastructure and training programs. Besides, there is also empirical evidence that Learning Analytics Tools (LATs) can also improve decision-making in higher education by providing data on student learning and engagement (Mukred et al., 2024). In this study, the Technology Acceptance Model (TAM) has been used to identify factors such as perceived usefulness, training and big data facilities, which are important for the successful adoption of LAT. These factors impact evidence-based decision-making in today's digital era.

2.3 Conceptual Model for LA

Lim (2021) used a conceptual model depicted in Figure 2.1 to explore inductively the theoretical framework on LA and its benefits from the perspective of knowledge and issues in students' learning processes and outcomes, learning

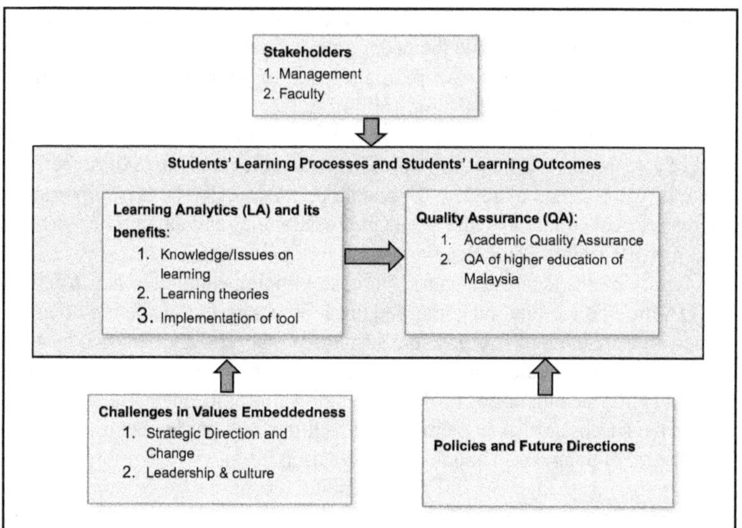

Figure 2.1 Conceptual Framework of Study

Source: AVCI et al., 2015; Bates, 2015; Hofer & Pintrich, 2011; Knight et al., 2014; Papamitsiou et al., 2014; Thille et al., 2017; West et al., 2018; Lew et al., 2013; Mokhtar et al., 2014; Kapur, 2018

theories and their implementation; QA from the perspective of academic QA and QA of HEIs in Malaysia; stakeholders from the perspectives of the management team and faculty members; and the challenges of value embeddedness and the emerging policies and directions of Malaysian higher education.

LA has been a hot topic for a while in the education industry. The effective use of data and LA is a critical component of a digital learning strategy to personalize instruction for many more students, particularly to increase students' achievement at the tertiary level. Having to measure against the achievement of QA of higher education in Malaysia, have the leaders in HEIs responded to this new phenomenon? Is LA going to bring us to higher QA in HEIs? "What is expected and how do we prepare students for jobs that have yet to be created as the current skill set could only last for the 'next 2 decades?'" Quadri and Shukor (2021) in their study highlight the benefits of LA in higher education for stakeholders such as students, faculty and administrators. LA's benefits include predicting student success, improving curriculum design and monitoring student engagement, which eventually encourage an effective learning environment. There are also many more students' issues on learning, which will be addressed in the following chapter.

To determine to what extent LA achieves QA, Lim (2021) zoomed on the understanding of knowledge/issues of student learning, learning theories and the LA implementation tool where the benefits of LA are ultimately the goal of the LA process impacting students' learning processes and students' learning outcomes. According to Dix and Leavesley (2015), the main components to be measured in LA include the pedagogy in the learning environment, such as adjustment of students' own path and pace of learning; type of learning-tailored instruction; and real-time formative feedback between students and instructors. Students' performance through assessment will then be the final goal of LA process. AI helps in improving assessments in terms of objectivity, scalability and personalization (Mohamad & Nazlan, 2024). It is important to address ethical concerns with respect to fairness, bias and data privacy, as well as to provide training and clear standards for responsible AI usage.

Identifying the determinants for successful implementation of LA in achieving QA may be the final outcome, requiring assessing the mediating effects of value embeddedness of LA to ensure sustainable success. As identified by Macfadyen et al. (2014), there are needs for a shift in the culture, technology infrastructure and teaching norms in HEIs, wherein value embeddedness is the key to ensure the success of LA implementation. All this will be discussed later in the last chapter of this book. Though there have been instances of slower processing and variation in predictions, the LSTM model has proven to be more accurate (Gnoh et al., 2024). It is important to ensure high accuracy in forecasting student enrollment, since university management depends on such prediction to make informed decisions about staffing, resources and educational quality, which contributes to UN Sustainable Development Goals (SDGs) of Decent Work and Quality Education. In this regard, Goal 4 and Goal 8 of SDG goals in particular ensure inclusive education and promoting economic growth respectively.

As HEIs are an example of a highly complex adaptive system, and we are going into an age in which learning might happen anyway, this study will culminate in the formulation of a novel strategic planning framework, collaborative policy development and leadership approach aimed at optimizing the education system for QA. A clear and precise conceptualization of the impact of LA on enhancing QA in higher education is essential; additionally, the stakeholders' resistance to change and adaptability toward LA significantly influence the establishment of a positive relationship. Rick (2013) stated that by supposing conflict to modification and preparing for it right from the beginning of the modification process, objections may be reduced. Hence, change and other challenges are crucial for institutions to embrace and implement the tool of LA for its benefits to students, staff and other stakeholders. Furthermore, stakeholders' flexibility to the new reality of the significant impact of digital technology on education is essential. Zhou and Lin (2016) cited Ployhart and Bliese's (2006) definition of suppleness as an individual's ability and willingness to adapt to changing tasks, social situations, or environments. Lee et al. (2023) identify many projects in Singapore using AI for personalized learning, enhancing students' engagement, optimizing resource allocation and predicting students' learning outcomes and success. Highlighting the advantages, the study also acknowledges limitations, which include further research to leverage AI and LA's potential fully so that it can improve teaching and learning in Singapore.

2.3.1 Quality Concept and Quality Assurance

QA from the perspective of tertiary education is defined in several ways. According to Kahveci et al. (2012), QA pertains to the process of sustaining values by placing benchmarks of attainment in a course, program or organization in a reliable and consistent manner. According to the definition of the Finnish Higher Evaluation Council, QA refers to the actions and practices of systems utilized by the HEIs to safeguard and enhance the value of its education and other goings-on (FINHEEC, 2008). Conferring to Brittingham (2009), QA is an expression of the higher education fraternity of what HEIs need to do so as to warrant community confidence where quality improvement is a framework for institutional development and self-evaluation; Vroeijenstijn (1995) also said that QA is the obligation of every person in higher education, from the highest administration to the junior staff members. This is further supported by NAAC and COL (2007), who define QA in terms of four components. These components indicate that one and all in the institution have a responsibility to enhance the value of products or services, maintain the quality of products and services, understand and sense the rights associated with the systems for maintaining the quality, and ensure that management regularly checks the validity of the system for quality control.

Conversely, Bowden and Marton, as cited by Srikanthan and Dalrymple (2002), assert that quality is attained by implementing the basic functions of research, community service and teaching. The main procedure for all the mentioned purposes is "learning", which encompasses all levels of participants, including students, researchers and the community. Learning helps students to handle unforeseen future circumstances based on present knowledge. An "ideal system" should incorporate the learning insights in academic programs and systems, as cited by Srikanthan and Dalrymple (2002) in Ewell (1997). These insights include transforming students, learner as an epistemologist, learning chance, learning well from the perspective of difficulties, response and learning in an interpersonal context.

Various terms and practices of QA were used in the assessment process (Srikanthan & Dalrymple, 2002) to evaluate quality in universities, emphasizing the need to measure and evaluate performance in terms of accountability of the institution. Reflecting on Harvey (1995), governments globally are considering higher education to respond more rapidly to economic and social needs, enhance access at reduced costs and ensure comparability among institutions. In other words, value has been utilized as a tool to safeguard compliance. In line with that, ISO 9000 standard is one of the well-known models for managing quality in higher education today (Harvey, 1995). It is an exterior standard which lays down a Quality Assurance System that must be followed by individuals involved in course provision. Its purpose is to maintain the quality of various course-related activities, ensuring that all courses are designed to meet student requirements and that processes are operational and well-organized.

As a whole, quality is important, whether in relation to goods or rendering services, and could never be over-emphasized. Especially in higher education, QA is of boundless significance to organizations, and there are diverse procedures for making sure quality services are delivered to the people. Common devices are accreditation, audits and assessment (Van Der Bank & Popoola, 2014). According to the British Standards Institution (BSI, 1991), QA could be categorized into three key components: relevance, standards and quality. These components encompass the various types and features of a service or product that adhere to its ability to meet the implied or stated needs. On this, the South African Qualification Authority Act (Act No. 58 of 1995) also terms the unit standards as the recorded testimonials of the sought-after education and training results and their related valuation standards. Quality is characterized as the expected performance, while relevance signifies that the content delivered must align with the aspirations and requirements of all standards, qualifications and users.

As stated earlier, the MQA oversees local qualifications and the accreditation, supervision, and regulation of higher education programs. The five clusters of the MQF serve as a principal benchmark to clarify the academic levels of learning outcomes. These clusters are knowledge and understanding; cognitive skills; functional work skills with focus on practical skills, interpersonal skills, communication skills, digital skills, numeracy skills, leadership, autonomy and responsibility; personal and entrepreneurial skills; and ethics and professionalism (MQA, 2017). As has been contended by Brennan and Shah (2000), the meaning of QA is comparable to academic ideals and is constant with evolving emphasis in higher education guidelines on students' learning outcomes on the precise stages of knowledge, abilities and skills that students attain as a result of their commitment in a specific education program. In local context, COPPA and COPIA have also been developed to benchmark international good practices in Malaysia (MQA, 2013).

The massification of higher education in Malaysia, impact on technology innovation, melodramatic alteration in social successes and change in occupation prospects have created new underlying forces influencing student learning engagement globally. Implementing OBE in all higher education programs, as exemplified by (MQA, 2013), involves aligning courses, modules and tasks within the current program structure with the overarching framework of continuous quality improvement (CQI) to ensure QA in higher education (MQA, 2013). The transition from prescriptive-based education to OBE is an ongoing process. Nevertheless, it is essential to develop lesson plans and lecturer notes that integrate content objectives, Study Learning Time (SLT) and performance indicators aligned with assessment instruments. This process must involve computational methods that utilize both traditional data and new data types from transferable systems within our existing learning management. On this note, LA initiatives play the utmost important role in this context. Hooda and Rana (2020) in their research examine which LA techniques are most effective for numerous challenges – finding applications in areas such as prediction of student performance, curriculum design and improving student engagement. The findings also include challenges such as data privacy and the need for ethical frameworks as LA evolves.

2.3.2 Stakeholder Theory

There is abundant literature on theories of stakeholders, including their features and attributes. Building on the study of Avci et al. (2015), the researchers refer to Burrows' (1999) numerous lenses method and Mitchell, Agle and Wood's (1997) theory of stakeholder identification and salience. Burrows' (1999) framework to classify stakeholders in HEIs suggests numerous lenses for distinguishing between stakeholders based on location (i.e., internal and external stakeholders), participation status (i.e., active or passive), possibility of collaboration and intimidation, and stakeholders' stake and influences on the institutions. Mitchell et al. (1997) suggested a theory of stakeholder credential and salience that comprises conceptions of power, legitimacy and urgency.

According to Mitchell et al. (1997), power is "a relationship among social actors in which one social action, A, can get another social actor B to do something that B would not have otherwise done" (p. 869). Lawfulness denotes the actions carried out based on the culture of society; urgency is related to stakeholders' plea for instant consideration; and the development of salience relates to the extent to which an action is prioritized. Big data analytics provides great opportunities for improving higher education by facilitating improved strategic planning and informing personalized learning approaches for students (Tasmin et al., 2020). However, choosing the right analytics tools remain as a challenge in integrating data sources to maximize the benefits for various stakeholders, such as educators, students and policymakers. Besides, Ismail et al. (2021) in their study employ LA to analyze student data and identify factors influencing engagement with LMS. The findings of the study recommended an important takeaway: that is, instructors play a key role in driving LMS engagement, and LA tools offer promising methods to improve students' motivation in learning as well as overall LMS effectiveness.

On closer examination, it becomes clear dealing with each stakeholder group requires a different approach. For example, students have the right to act as internal shareholders, faculty and staff own the institution, management is interested in maintaining its financial stability, and experts and government have political interests (Mitchell, et al., 1997). On the other hand, in keeping the dynamic features of the salience of stakeholders in the instances where governments make rules and guidelines, the government also has a pressing need to establish itself as an authoritative stakeholder. With that, the management and faculty, who have key influence in strategic, financial, and academic affairs, are considered stakeholders of higher education institutions (HEIs). However, due to the complex nature of HEIs, identifying all stakeholders can be challenging. For instance, a study by Ateeq et al. (2024) examines the benefits of AI to improve university education. The findings highlight the importance of addressing faculty readiness and ethical considerations for AI use in education while AI tools can enhance personalized learning, writing and research skills.

2.4 Conclusion

Reviews were done based on the domain of effect on teaching and learning in line with the conceptualization of the framework of study: that is, how learning theories have been developed where pedagogies of LA framework can be grounded to achieve maximum gain to support students' learning processes. The theory of behaviorist learning, theory of cognitive learning; theory of constructivist and theory of connectivism were reviewed. Moreover, a conceptual model was adopted where all relevant theories and concepts related to the aspects of study were reviewed.

References

Abdul Jalil, N., Nasir, A., & Wong Ei Leen, M. (2021). Learning analytics in higher education: The student expectations of learning analytics. In *Proceedings of the 2021 5th international conference on education and e-learning* (pp. 142–147). Institute of Electrical and Electronics Engineers (IEEE).

Arvinth, A. (2024). Effects of Artificial Intelligence on Academics in Higher Education in India: An Empirical Study. *International Journal of Novel Research and Development*, *9*(5), 1–10. Retrieved from IJNRD2405255.

Ateeq, A., Alshahrani, M., Alzahrani, A., & Alharthi, M. (2024). Empowering academic success: Integrating AI tools in university teaching for enhanced assignment and thesis guidance. In *2024 ASU international conference in emerging technologies for sustainability and intelligent systems(ICETSIS)* (pp. 1–6). Institute of Electrical and Electronics Engineers (IEEE).

Avci, O., Ring, E., & Mitchelli, L. (2015). Stakeholders in U.S. higher education: An analysis through two theories of stakeholders. *The Journal of Knowledge Economy & Knowledge Management*, *X*(Fall).

Bates, A. W. (2015). Teaching in a digital age – Guidelines for designing teaching and learning. *Creative commons attribution-non-commercial 4.0 international license*. https://bccampus.ca/open-textbook-project/

Behrens, J. T., Carlisle, J. M., & Steinmetz, A. (2010). The impact of robotics on student motivation and engagement in science and engineering. *International Journal of Technology in Education*, *14*(3), 187–204.

Boss, S. (2011, September 20). *Project-based learning: A short history*. https://www.edutopia.org/project-based-learning-history

Brennan, J., & Shah, T. (2000). *Managing quality in higher education: An international perspective on institutional assessment and change*. Buckingham, England: Society for Research into Higher Education & Open University Press.

British Standard Institution. (1991). *Quality vocabulary part 2: Quality concepts and related definitions*. BSI.

Brittingham, B. (2009, August 20). Quality assurance in higher education. USAID/EGAT/ED. *Worldwide education and training workshop*. Washington, DC: USAID.

Burrow, J. (1999). Going beyond labels: A framework for profiling institutional stakeholders. *Contemporary Education*, *70*(4), 5–10.

Campbell, S. W. (2002). The role of robotics in K-12 education: A review of the literature. *International Journal of Technology in Education*, *1*(1), 1–17.

Cherry, K. (2018). *An overview of behavioral psychology*. https://www.verywellmind.com/behavioral-psychology-4157183

Dahri, N. A., Awan, U., & Ali, S. (2024). Investigating AI-based academic support acceptance and its impact on students' performance in Malaysian and Pakistani higher education institutions. *Education and Information Technologies*, 1–50.

David, L. (2015). *"Social learning theory (Bandura)," in learning theories*. https://www.learning-theories.com/social-learning-theory-bandura.html

Dix, A., & Leavesley, J. (2015). *Learning analytics for the academics: An action perspective*. http://alandix.com/academic/papers/JUCS-action-analytics-2015/jucs_action_analytics-2015.pdf

Ferguson, R. (2012). *Social learning analytics*. https://www.slideshare.net/R3beccaF/social-learning-analytics-lak-2012

Ferriman, J. (2017). *Three instructional design theory*. https://www.learndash.com/3-instructional-design-theories/

FINHEEC. (2008). Audits of quality assurance system of Finnish higher education institutions, audit manual for 2008–2011. *Finish higher education evaluation council*. www.kka.fi/files/147/KKA_1007.pdf

Gnoh, H. Q., Keoy, K. H., Iqbal, J., Anjum, S. S., Yeo, S. F., Lim, A. F., ... & Chaw, L. Y. (2024). Enhancing business sustainability through technology-enabled AI: Forecasting student data and comparing prediction models for higher education institutions (HEIs). *PaperASIA*, *40*(2b), 48–58.

Gutierrez, K. (2015). *Overall overview of 4 instructional design model*. https://www.shiftelearning.com/blog/top-instructional-design-models-explained

Hamzah, H. A., & Abu Seman, M. S. (2024). Existing quality assurance frameworks for online learning platforms. *Kurdish Studies*, *12*(2), 2181–2192.

Haron, N. H., Ahmad, A., & Rahman, M. (2025). An artificial intelligence approach to monitor and predict student academic performance. *Journal of Advanced Research in Applied Sciences and Engineering Technology*, *44*(1), 105–119.

Harvey, L. (1995). *Quality assurance system, TQM and the new collegialism: Center for research into quality*. University of Central England.

Hofer, B.K., & Pintrich, P.R. (1997). The Development of Epistemological Theories: Belief about Knowledge and Knowing and the Relations to Learning. *Review of Educational Research, 67*, 88. doi: 10.3102/00346543067001088.

Hoffmann, J., Schunn, C. D., & Pea, R. D. (2015). The impact of robotics on student learning: A meta-analysis. *Journal of Educational Psychology*, *107*(3), 394–407.

Hooda, M., & Rana, C. (2020). Learning analytics lens: Improving quality of higher education. *International Journal of Emerging Trends in Engineering Research*, *8*(5), 1023–1028.

Ismail, S.N., Annamalai, N., & Ramayah, T. (2021). Exploring students' engagement towards the learning management system (LMS) using learning analytics. *Computer Systems Science & Engineering*, *37*(1), 181–192.

Jou, B., Hsu, C.-H., & Chang, C.-C. (2010). The effectiveness of robotics education in elementary schools: A meta-analysis. *International Journal of Technology in Education*, *14*(2), 101–116.

Kahveci, T. C., Uygun, O., Yurtsever, U., & Ilyas, S. (2012). Quality assurance in higher education institutions using strategic information system. International conference on New Horizons in education INTE2012. Elseview Ltd. *Social and Behavioral Sciences*, *55*(2012), 161–167. https://ac.els-cdn.com/S1877042812039523/1-s2.0-S1877042812039523-main.pdf?_tid=f60097fe-84e6-43df-b5eb-afba57505d2d&acdnat=1540069099_febdc92d631544ed80ab7da7ac6ba3d5

Kapur, R. (2018). *Educational Leadership*. ResearchGate. Retrieved from https://www.researchgate.net/publication/323691649_Educational_Leadership

Knight, S., Buckingham Shum, S., & Littleton, K. (2014). Epistemology, assessment, pedagogy: Where learning meets analytics in the middle space. *Journal of Learning Analytics*, *1*(2). http://epress.lib.uts.edu.au/journals/index.php/JLA/article/view/3538

Kurkovsky, S. (2014). Robotics education: A review of the literature. *International Journal of Technology in Education, 18*(2), 117–132.

Lee, A. V. Y., Koh, E., & Looi, C. K. (2023). AI in education and learning analytics in Singapore: An overview of key projects and initiatives. *Information and Technology in Education and Learning*, *3*(1), Inv–p001.

Lim. (2021). *Learning analytics towards achieving quality assurance: A case study of private university in Kuala Lumpur* [Unpublished doctoral dissertation, University Malaya].

Macfadyen, L. P., Awson, S., Pardo, A., & Gasevic, D. (2014). Embracing big data in complex educational system: The learning analytics imperative and policy challenge. *Research & Practice in Assessment*, *9*(4), 17–28. http://www.rpajournal.com/dev/wp-content/uploads/2014/10/A2.pdf

Malaysian Qualifications Agency. (2013). *Malaysian qualifications framework (MQF)*. Malaysian Qualifications Agency Malaysia (MQA).

Malaysian Qualifications Agency. (2017). *Malaysian qualifications framework (MQF)* (2nd ed.). http://pps.utem.edu.my/phocadownloadpap/2018%20MQF%202nd%20Edition%2002042018.pdf

Malaysian Qualifications Agency. (2018a). *Code of practice for programme accreditation*. http://www.moh.gov.my/images/gallery/Garispanduan/Guidelines On Approval And Accreditation Of Optometry And Op.pdf

Malaysian Qualifications Agency. (2018b). *COPIA form. MQA-03 (self-review portfolio)*(2nd ed.). http://www.mqa.gov.my/portalMQAv3/borang/copia/MQA-03 (2nd Edition).pdf

Mitchell, R. K., Agle, B. R., & Wood, D. J. (1997). *Towards a theory of stakeholder identification and salience: Defining the principle of who and what really counts*. http://www.jstor.org/stable/pdfplus/259247.pdf

Mohamad, S. N. A., & Nazlan, N. H. (2024). The educator's dilemma: Balancing AI advancements with ethical concerns in assessments for higher education. *International Journal of e-Learning and Higher Education (IJELHE)*, *19*(2), 73–91.

Mokhtar, R., Rahman, A.A., Othman S.H., & Ali, N. (2014). Malaysian Academic Quality Assurance System in the context of issues, challenges and best practices. Knowledge Management International Conference (KMICe). *Research Gate Malaysia*, 12–15. Retrieved from https://www.researchgate.net/publication/267633436_Malaysian_Academic_Quality_AssuranceSystem_in_the_context_of_issues_challenges_and_best_practices?_esc=publicationCoverPdf&el=1_x_3&enrichId=rgreq-691dccb67fac0146c7a8eb08a4ddb8fe-XXX&enrichSource=Y292ZXJQYWdlOzI2NzYzMzQzNjtBUzoxNTg4ODc3MDEzOTM0MDhAMTQxNDg5MzE4ODY0OA%3D%3D

Mukred, M., et al. (2024). The Effectiveness of Educational Robots in Improving Learning Outcomes: A Meta-Analysis. *Sustainability*, *15*(5), 4637. Retrieved from https://www.mdpi.com/2071-1050/15/5/4637.

NAAC & COL. (2007). *Quality assurance in higher education*. National Assessment and Accreditation Council, India, Commonwealth of Learning, Canada.

Omar, Z.-F., Mior Harun, M., Mohd Ishar, N. I., Mustapha, N. A., & Ismail, Z. (2024a). Enhancing professional development and training through AI for personalized learning: A framework to engaging learners. *International Journal of e-Learning and Higher Education (IJELHE)*, *19*(3), 115–138.

Omar, Z.-F., Mior Harun, M., Mohd Ishar, N. I., Mustapha, N. A., & Ismail, Z. (2024b). Leveraging artificial intelligence for enhancing postgraduate teaching: A framework to engaging professional learners. *International Journal of e-Learning and Higher Education (IJELHE)*, *19*(2), 177–196.

Papamitsiou, Z., & Economides, A. A. (2014). Learning analytics: A systematic review of the literature. *Educational Technology & Society*, *17*(4), 1–14.

Quadri, A., & Shukor, N. (2021). The benefits of learning analytics to higher education institutions: A scoping review. *International Journal of Emerging Technologies in Learning (iJET)*, *16*(23), 4–15.

Rahiman, H. U., & Kodikal, R. (2024). Revolutionizing education: Artificial intelligence empowered learning in higher education. *Cogent Education*, *11*(1), 2293431.

Rick, T. (2013). *Resistant to change is a problem*. https://www.torbenrick.eu/blog/change-management/change-is-not-the-problem-resistance-to-change-is-the-problem/

Siemens, G. (2004). Connectivism: A learning theory for the digital age. *Ekim*, *6*, 2011.

Srikanthan, G., & Dalrymple, J. F. (2002). Developing a holistic model for quality in higher education. *Quality in Higher Education*, *8*(3), 215–224. https://doi.org/10.1080/1353832022000031656. https://pdfs.semanticscholar.org/e6ec/9e984214bab5b298488f41442a095660ffd1.pdf?_ga=2.209295131.843471868.1540443894-1757868047.1540443894

Sutton, R. S., & Barto, A. G. (2017). *Reinforcement learning: An introduction* (2nd ed.). MIT Press. http://incompleteideas.net/book/bookdraft2017nov5.pdf

Tasmin, R., Muhammad, R. N., & Nor Aziati, A. H. (2020). Big data analytics applicability in higher learning educational system. In *IOP conference series: Materials science and engineering* (Vol. 917, No. 1, p. 012023). IOP Publishing.

Thille, C., & Zimmaro, D. (2017). Incorporating Learning Analytics in the Classroom. In Zilvinskis J., Boarder V. 2017. Learning Analytics in Higher Education. *New Directions for Higher Education. 179* (Fall). Jossey-Bass San Francisco.

Ullah, H., Rehman, A. U., & Bibi, S. (2015). Gagne's 9 events of instruction – a time tested way to improve teaching. *Pakistan Armed Forces Medical Journal*, *65*(4), 535–539. http://pafmj.org/pdfs/August-2015/Article_23.pdf

Van Der Bank, C. M., & Popoola, B. A. (2014). A theoretical framework of total quality assurance in university of technology. *Academic Journal of Interdisciplinary Studies*, MCSER Publishing, Rome Italy. www.mcser.org/journal/index.php/ajis/article/viewFile/3117/3073

Vroeijenstijn, A. I. (1995). *Quality assurance in higher education: A study of the quality assurance system of Dutch higher education institutions*. Netherlands: The Netherlands Organization for International Cooperation in Higher Education (Nuffic).

West, D., Luzeckyj, A., Tasir, Z., Toohey, D.P. (2018). Learning analytics experience among academics in Australia and Malaysia: A comparison. *34*(3). doi: 10.14742ajet.3836. 122–139.

Williams, M. K. (2017). John Dewey in the 21st century. *Journal of Inquiry & Action in Education*, *9*(1), 91–102. https://files.eric.ed.gov/fulltext/EJ1158258.pdf

Yang, Y., Chen, L., & Wang, H. (2024). Investigation and the development of learning analytics dashboard in open and distance learning using big data mining. *Journal of Autonomous Intelligence*, *7*(5), 1–12.

Zhou, M., & Brown, D. (2015). *Educational learning theories*. https://oer.galileo.usg.edu/cgi/viewcontent.cgi?referer=&httpsredir=1&article=1000&context=education-textbooks

Zhou, M., & Lin, W. (2016). Adaptability and life satisfaction: The moderating role of social support. *Frontiers in Psychology*, *7*(1134). https://doi.org/10.3389/fpsyg.2016.01134. https://www.ncbi.nlm.nih.gov/pmc/articles/PMC4963457/

Zhou, T., & Lin, X. (2016). The role of suppleness in adapting to task and environmental changes. *Journal of Organizational Behavior*, *37*(4), 500–520.

3 Epistemological Reflection on Current Issues of Students' Learning Processes and Learning Outcomes

3.1 Introduction

In line with the background and the conceptualization of the framework of the study, the chapter explains LA and its epistemological implications for current issues of learning that stakeholders face, emphasizing that the effective use of data in LA is a critical component to increase students' graduate attributes.

LA is such an emergent technological practice aimed at facilitating effective learning and teaching outcomes – that is, knowledge. LA consists of the use of a wide range of data and procedures for analysis, such as statistical tests and predictive and data visualization models (Arroway et al., 2016). Although the use of data in HEIs is undoubtedly old, the computer procedures involved in forming it for expectation, involvement and keeping track have stretched out incredibly recently. Campbell et al. (2007, p. 42) wrote, "Analytics marries large datasets, statistical techniques, and predictive modeling". LA utilizes both outmoded data (i.e., from student enrollment surveys, records and others) and new forms of data originating from transactional methods such as LMS, online courses and other linkages. Hence, in this context of study, LA is defined by Zilvinskis et al. (2017, p. 10) as the process of using live data collected to predict student success, promote intervention or support based on those predictions and monitor the influence of that action. In general, as emphasized by Avella et al. (2016) on the benefits of implementing LA, it is perceived to circle around planned course offerings, curriculum development, students' learning outcomes, behavioral processes, personalized learning, enhancements in lecturer performances, prospects for post-educational jobs, as well as educational research improvements.

To recap on the conceptualization of this study, the benefits of LA are to be measured by the EPA Triad, which illustrates the theoretical interconnections inherent in our pedagogical and valuation procedures and guidelines and their fundamental epistemological repercussions and expectations (Knight et al., 2014). The theory of "knowledge" is thus to be reviewed in relation to issues of learning and teaching reflecting the local context. Lemos (2007) stated that the theory of knowledge (epistemology) is one of the cornerstones

DOI: 10.4324/9781003584520-3

of philosophy. In fact, some of the issues are as old as Plato, as written by Lemos (2007); however, they stay alive and thought-provoking nowadays. For example, Theaetetus is one of Plato's discourses regarding the nature of knowledge. In addition, according to Hofer and Pintrich (1997), knowledge theory is a subject of philosophy on human knowledge's nature and reasoning. Hence, educators are increasingly aware of the development of personal and epistemological principles in people's discovery process, the concepts and views they possess about awareness and the way in which such epistemological principles are part of and have an effect on the cognitive practices of discerning and reasoning. So, what is knowledge?

According to Biggam (2001), it is extensively acknowledged by the researchers and practitioners that they have been unsuccessful in reaching an agreement on the meaning of what forms knowledge. Hence, to enhance the knowledge of LA and its benefits, it is essential to interpret the term "knowledge", which was built on a solid foundation such that it must be correct, the perceiver must trust this to be the case and the perceiver must be in a spot to identify this to be the case. Researchers will then have a better view on understanding LA and its contribution to higher student learning success. Implicitly, Hofer and Pintrich (1997) concluded in their article on epistemological theories that current shifts in educational thinking towards a constructivist approach and beyond will undoubtedly continue to influence research in this field, influencing students' and instructors' perceptions of facts and their understanding of knowledge, which in turn will enhance the understanding of teaching and learning processes in HEIs.

3.2 Rising Cost of Learning Leads to Incompletion of Programs

The cost of a tertiary education obviously determines the price that individuals pay in the form of tuition. As tuition fees have risen, rendering learning inaccessible, the initial step in tackling this rise in costs is to seek solutions to combat the "cost disease", betting to close the affordability gap possibly by technology, which will dominate the economics of higher education in the foreseeable future (Brown, 2011).

One example is the launch of MOOC and online learning to enhance its affordability. According to Brown (2011), online learning is now broadly accepted in the initiation of LMS, with the most significant change in online learning today coming from LMS in LA. However, no one has devised the magic formulation for how HEIs can use LA to gain competitive advantage on their capability to use online learner actions to forecast students' performance in class, whereby the rate of incompletion of programs can be reduced. Well, it is well-documented that executing and maintaining LA practices are just not easy, as the more intricate characteristics of higher education are being addressed, despite the helpful new technologies and methods, which have indirectly resulted in far-fetched variety and intricacy of learning outcomes (Zilvinskis et al., 2017). So, will LA be one of the critical components of a digital learning strategy to personalize instruction for many more students, whether in online or face-to-face learning, particularly to increase students' achievements at the tertiary level of education in Malaysia?

3.3 Learning Digital Literacy to Integrate Formal and Informal Learning Approaches

The Horizon reports noted in Elmes (2017) that being digitally literate is more than attaining remote technical abilities. It is about creating an abysmal comprehension of the digital setting, allowing instinctual variation to new situations and co-designing subject matter with others (Elmes, 2017). HEIs have no choice but to be held responsible for developing students' digital citizenship – not only to ensure the right usage of technology but also to be a responsible and ethical user.

Elmes (2017) stated that higher education leaders face challenges in gaining organization-wide support and maintaining all stakeholders' interest in being digital savvy due to the abundance of components involved. However, the report also records that while countless programs in digital literacy are in their implementation process, instead of adopting what "everyone's talking about", one should exercise caution before diving in as there will be tremendous comprehensive ownerships and actions needed. It is interesting to find out what will hinder the use of technology in higher education five years from now. LA relies on digital data that is captured in systems related to the educational journey; hence, responses to the institutional capacity in supporting LA are to be looked at and thus become a coherent effort for achieving QA in higher education.

Leadership in conventional education policy has been repeatedly proven successful over the past centuries. However, change in higher education is real; impactful data suggests that technology has been steadily changing assessment regimes, related pedagogies and associated epistemologies (Elmes, 2017). Professionals believe that combining formal and informal approaches of learning could generate a situation that nurtures conducting tests, inquisitiveness and creativeness. The 2017 testimony reiterates Elmes (2017) that a predominant aim is to nurture the quest for permanent learning in all learners and academicians. As such, HEIs are starting to experiment with adaptable programs that make available credit for previous learning and proficiencies obtained through jobs or experiences in extracurriculars.

Elmes (2017) cautions warns that, first, the lack of workable procedures for keeping records formally and assessing skills learned out of the lecture hall and, second, the adaptation of price listings and monetary assistance models to better suit the new degree choices are both hampering progress. While the HEIs are distinctively positioned to "join more learners" to informal opportunities, the European Commission is also configuring a persuasive policy practice by distinctively positioning non-formalized learning endorsement, which escalates the distinguishability of learning outcomes and the right value of these experiences (Elmes, 2017). Learning theories, to a great extent, have to be extended and reconstructed over place and time. There will be continuous exploration of epistemological tradition in relation to learning, whereby one has to justify if knowledge is gained through experience, in this case hands-on experiences during an internship, or if reality is internal, where knowledge is constructed as per the interpretivist via the real-time feedback adaptive learning platform (Elmes, 2017).

3.4 Knowledge Management

Questions normally raised in higher education these days for discussion are as follows: Has anyone ever described how assessment services determine whether or not the information and skills students are learning now will peak in ten years? What if employers begin to recognize students' expertise beyond what universities certify through the degrees they traditionally grant? Challenges arise when there is a discrepancy between employer demands and the competence available to do the duties, or when the supply and demand for HR do not align. So how can HEIs ensure that the graduates coming out of their curricula are the right kind of graduates, ready for a progressively unpredictable, undefined, intricate future? (Bates, 2015)

In a digital era where we are wrapped up in technology maneuvering to enormous transformation in the economy, one of the main challenges faced by HEIs is the rising demand for knowledge, which is becoming an increasingly vital component of economic growth and, most importantly, in the creation of employment (Bates, 2015). Consequently, the kinds of skills and knowledge needed of graduates change too. According to Bates (2015), it is rather difficult to predict what graduates will be actually doing after graduation, except in a broad term. It is because the knowledge base and even working environments are expected to go through speedy change and conversion over time.

Cited in Bates (2015), according to Scardamalia and Bereiter (2003), knowledge building is a "collective cognitive responsibility", wherein learning is an inner, imperceptible process may alter that skills, attitudes or beliefs as a result, whereas knowledge building by divergence will result in the formation of public knowledge. Bates (2015) wrote that knowledge involves content and skills. The concern is not the fact that teachers do not assist learners in skill development, regardless of whether these skills align with the aspirations of knowledge-based employees, even if sufficient emphasis is placed on skill improvement within the curriculum. This study coherently aims to explore how LA enhances the understanding of students' learning processes and improves learning outcomes.

One of the main skills included by Bates (2015) in his book is managing knowledge. Knowledge is rapidly evolving due to new research and development, while the sources of information are constantly proliferating.. Hence, the knowledge learnt in a university by a student can quickly become obsolete. Bates (2015) emphasized that the vital skill in a knowledge-established culture is the ability to discover, assess, examine, put on and distribute information within a specific perspective so that graduates are able to employ these skills long after graduation. This undoubtedly impacts the instructional material and methodology to ensure that students graduate with the requisite knowledge and abilities for the digital age.

Looking from the lens of the notion of realism on the other hand, is getting a degree from a university the only way to get ahead in life? Bates (2015) highlighted that emphasizing the skills necessary in a digital era raises questions regarding the motivations of universities, specifically whether the objective of HEIs is to produce job-ready graduates for the workforce. Is university education intended to focus on personal growth and information acquisition, as well as broadening one's perspectives, rather than solely preparing individuals for employment? Bates (2015) asserted that the organization of proficient staff has consistently been a responsibility of colleges, since employers and parents seek a workforce that is employable, competitive, and potentially affluent.

Think about who will benefit the most. In the opinion of researchers, it all depends again on what one wants in life. One exists merely to facilitate one's own existence, or one aspires to excel in societal endeavors and dominate the competition. In this study, the coordinated efforts of LA to achieve QA in higher education in Malaysia contribute to knowledge creation and management..

Fischer (2000) state, "Learning can no longer be dichotomized into a place and time to acquire knowledge (school) and a place and time to apply knowledge (workplace)" (p. 3). As we are swamped with extra information than we can grip, and tomorrow's workforces must know more than any individual can maintain, lifelong learning is thus an important test for devising the future of our societies. Fischer (2000) has further emphasized that lifetime learning transcends education for adults; it embodies a mindset and practices essential for societal achievement. It indeed forms the dares to comprehend, to discover and to upkeep the new necessary scopes of learning, such as self-directed learning, learning on request, learning collaboratively and organizational learning, where these methods need new means and state-of-the-art technologies to be sufficiently backed.

Fischer (2000) in his research concluded that lifelong learning is essentially a problem for our present-day and future data culture; regrettably, there are no easy responses and no easy truths that will permit itemizing for short-time failures and successes. Hence, to adopt a front-loading approach, inductively re-looking into continuous learning is the trend in learning today. How do we get there? In the opinion of researchers, there is no universal solution. Whether you like it or not, it has to be dealt with in the 4.0 millage management context we are in now. As said, everyone has a different way and perspective on what one wants. The researchers suppose setting a target using technology to digitize and automatize is the beginning. The challenge of learners being reluctant to learn is another to be overcome. Thus, continuing to emphasize on continuous education and listening to their views, we believe that the results of digitization cannot be much more difficult than before. Moreover, the implementation of LA in supporting knowledge management, reducing knowledge obsolescence and encouraging lifelong learning entails effective use of feedback and interventions, undoubtedly requiring a coordinated approach towards support, tracking and evaluation.

3.5 21st-Century Skills

Reported by the Future of Jobs Report 2020 (World Economic Forum, 2020), COVID-19 lockdowns and the global recession of 2020 have created a highly uncertain outlook for the employment market. The skills gap will remain large as skills demand will change by job category over the next five years. Top skills and groups that employers believe will be important by 2025 include groups such as critical thinking and analysis and problem-solving skills such as active learning, resilience, stress tolerance, flexibility and self-management. On average, companies estimate that about 40% of employees need reskilling within six months, and currently 94% of company managers expect their employees to acquire new skills on the job as compared to 65% in 2018 (World Economic Forum, 2020). Hence, as the need for transformation in our world is changing so fast, Elmes (2017) reported that the one method means – the traditional method of higher education are no longer sufficient to meet the needs of today's increasingly diverse student population. Coupled with the increasingly high tuition costs, supplementary degree procedures are desired.

Elmes (2017) added in the report that the task facing higher education is to tailor to all students' needs and develop parallel post-secondary programs that yield deeper learning results and the attainment of future skills, facilitated by personalized learning approaches and data-compelled learner backing arrangements that adopt objective realization and rewarding occupations. The report noted that online or blended offerings with "personalized and adaptive learning approaches" are more and more regarded as students' retention resolution. A case in point consists of the competency-based education method used by Western Governors University and Southern New Hampshire University, which targets to back achievement and employability by equipping online learners with relevant skills aligned with their career objectives (Elmes, 2017). Extrapolating from the current practice of higher learning institutions in the United States and globally, to boost student retention rates by facilitating the early identification of struggling students, thereby reducing attrition rates.

Students demand personalized learning experience (Elmes, 2017). As classrooms get larger and larger, students' learning processes need to be understood better, including progression in their journey. As such, a new phenomenon has emerged where LA is to improvise students' learning experience so as to meet end needs of future skills. But the issue is, "how do educators respond to this?" How do educators prepare students for the future of work, jobs that have yet to be created? Could current skill sets that exist now only last for "the next decade or two"?

To serve the students of today and the future is indeed the mission of all educationalists. Could the future of work be done anywhere, and the processing power of computers enable machines to outperform humans for an ever-increasing scope of work? That is a great challenge in learning today (Elmes, 2017). As far as curriculum and learning processes are concerned, people cannot work in vacuum, especially with new learning tools and new curriculum. Each phase and every module have to work toward solving the bigger and bigger challenge, with the involvement of students and other change agents. We need to change, but the questions are as follows: How do we adopt technology? How to move to the new material? How to integrate case studies in curriculum, and many more insights? An important role is played by policies and management, especially in the preparation stage, to encourage students to learn, especially those who are reluctant to learn new things.

In Malaysia, matrix of PLO against the Program Educational Objective (PEO) has to be developed, and PLOs are required to be met in accordance with the level of study in line with the MQF-level descriptors and the five-cluster MQF learning outcomes, as mentioned earlier (MQA, 2018a). Essentially, to effectively ensure competencies developed through the programs with LA will be holistic. For a business program for example, besides gaining knowledge in business theories and concepts, students are exposed to workplace competencies such as leadership, teamwork, communications and collaboration skills for group cooperation. Also, thinking critically and developing skills in solving problems through case studies and problem-based learning will prepare them for the real world later on, which includes development of abilities and attitudes toward integrating lifelong learning for career progression and meeting evolving needs.

3.6 Transfer of Knowledge

Education must be able to lead to empowerment (Granados, 2015). As educationists, we should ensure students learn so that they are able to attain the ability to create resolutions and carry them out successfully. Thus, students do not merely develop individual but also social merits; this entails the enhancement of social principles, fostering learning to be aware of how society works and how knowledge is structured between the individual and its organization collectively within shared and distinct well-being amid privileges and responsibilities (Granados, 2015). For seeing the realm and therefore education in a fresh way, Granados (2015) stated that higher education is confronting higher degree of trials. As a result, changes are expected in HEIs, such as focusing on the selection of data and communication technologies in the creation and dissemination of information. In a knowledge society and digital world, students should be facilitated to learn in a more active manner and also learn to be connected to real life. Whatever students learn must be relevant so that whatever is anticipated of them should be understood as a transmission of knowledge to the social order (Granados, 2015).

Therefore, where to learn needed knowledge? Elmes (2017) in the Horizon Report stated that it is challenging for academics to stay organized and relevant as educational needs, software and devices advance speedily. Even though high-tech improvements can possibly increase the value of learning and the processes at universities, the speed of keeping up with the newer versions is making sustainability an almost impossible task. Hence, there is an additional burden to make certain that any tools chosen are to deepen learning results in methods that are quantifiable, thereby addressing needs aligned with limited resources and ensuring QA, especially relating to the relevance of knowledge gain for the industry. In this context of study, it becomes coherent to see the extent to which LA tools achieve QA of higher education in the notion of students' learning and students' outcome.

Besides, Bates (2015) asserted that teaching methods that aid the development and transfer precise skills need to be used so that knowledge growth and distribution can be served while simultaneously getting graduates ready for employment in the knowledge-grounded culture. From a macro-perspective, educational learning models such as emphasizing internships into tertiary programs are made more acceptable, in fact encouraged by the Malaysian government – for example, the introduction of the 2u2i model, which mandates two years of industry experience as part of the curriculum for graduates. This initiative ensures that knowledge learned is transferred from the universities through a work-based learning program that encompasses areas of knowledge and understanding, thinking skills, practical skills, and general skills as outlined in the MQF domain (MQA, 2018b).

3.7 Response to New Method of Teaching and Curriculum

Organizations are preparing to assist educationalists change their teaching methods, thanks to the creative use of technology, (Gasevic et al., 2016). The Maryland University College is launching a three-year initiative to change its pedagogies from those centered on learning by heart-knowledge to experiential learning and competency – drastically altering the teaching culture. Academics and researchers have welcomed LA as one of the impending "game-changers" in HEIs. LA offers various types of calibrated computer backup for monitoring student conduct, mining scholastic information, envisioning configurations and quantifiably providing feedback to both educators and students to build competencies not only for students but also for education operators (Gasevic et al., 2016).

Furthermore, a more personalized learning experience is required as classrooms are getting larger these days and teachers need to understand students better as well as how students progress in their journey. Of the implementations utilizing varied methods for numerous objects, according to Gasevic et al. (2016), there are three major themes in LA execution: that is, the advance of predictors and gauges for several elements such as academic achievement, student engagement and self-controlled learning skills; the visualization to discover and deduce information and to prompt corrective arrangements; and, finally, the beginning of interventions to form the learning setting.

The issue is: How can academics get more involved in LA activity to improve student learning experience? West et al. (2018) conducted a study on LA experience among academics in Australia and Malaysia. Concerns about academics in Malaysia include their interest in LA, although it is yet a main concern or priority for most, and their preference for improving their own teaching, rather than focusing on how that determines attrition rate, which is seen as more of an institutional concern. Additionally, it has been revealed that only a small percentage of academics were engaged in discussion on LA with their colleagues. Why? Given LA is regarded as a catalyst for decision-making at all levels, as noted by Berneveld, Arnold and Campbell (2012), the research suggested a more introspective view of LA among academics in Malaysia, suggesting that a deeper understanding of its implications and applications could enhance educational practices and outcomes within the region. Accordingly, that may be influenced by the lack of LA adoption in institutions, or it may be due to the early stage of maturity of LA applications in many institutions (West et al., 2018).

3.8 Response to Quality of Teaching

Quality of teaching is the use of technique to deliver students' learning outcomes at institutional, program or individual levels. Different efforts at the nationwide and academic levels are performed to enhance the teaching excellence at institutions of higher education in Malaysia through endorsement of the program management and standardize student learning experience. Activities include support of innovative pedagogies and competency-based training (Henard & Roseveare, 2012). The question is, it does not promise excellent teaching inside the lecture room! Is the employees' growth often taking place to promote sustainable learning? If not, it will not have great impact on instructional practice. At university, establishing practicing groups in all faculties needs radical change in various areas, such as job description, cost effectiveness and many other interdependent constructs.

Why is there extensive effort in upgrading the teaching skills at the faculty level? As per Institutional Management in Higher Education (IMHE) report (Henard & Roseveare, 2012), HEIs must safeguard that the instruction they propose matches the anticipations of learners and the growing demand in desires of companies currently and in the future so that students are equipped with the skills required to progress professionally throughout lifetime. Instructional methods that align with the evolving expectations of learners and the increasing demands of employers must be uphold so that students are equipped with the essential skills needed for lifelong professional advancement.

The quality of teaching globally is also influenced by related shifts within the higher education surroundings (Henard & Roseveare, 2012). Aspects influencing the instructional quality consist of the internationalization of HEIs; the progressively widening range of education and greater mixture of leaners' biographies; the fast shifts in technology which could rapidly create program subject matter and pedagogics being outdated; the request for bigger public involvement of graduates and regionalized progression of HEIs; the augmented burden of worldwide rivalry and economic competency; and most importantly, the necessity to yield skilled employees to encounter the 21st-century challenges (Henard & Roseveare, 2012).

Educators have to validate that they are the dependable educational service providers of respectable class HEIs while functioning in an intricate situation with several stakeholders, each with their personal anticipations (government agencies, finance agencies, authorities and employers); to juggle their work accomplishments on teaching and learning alongside with research accomplishment, since top world-class universities, research accomplishments are not adequate to retain the status of the organization; to more efficiently strive for learners against the factors of greater tuition costs and larger learner movement; and to upsurge the competence of the teaching and learning progression as financial limitations become inflexible.

3.9 Capacity of Teachers on Teaching Practice for Learning Reform

Besides the notion of culture in respect to resistance to change and adaptability, strategic direction is utmost important as leadership will be the backbone of technology infrastructure. Also, teacher's capability in terms of how knowledge pedagogy differs in teaching practices which enable them to understand which algorithms and visualizations have the potential to be educationally valuable and to be redefined and redeveloped as new policies in Malaysia. The educator's role has transformed intensely in the new standard of teaching from the "sage on the stage" to the "guide on the side". Three key parts needed in being a facilitator are the followings: firstly, as a learner's task designer (Schlechty, 2002). The learner's tasks comprise carrying out both the task scope and the teaching scope. Secondly, the instructor is an initiator of the learning procedures. This consists of assisting to do up an individual study plan, tutoring or rearranging the learner's learning when needed, aiding dialogue and thinking back, and positioning ease of use of numerous human and material assets. Thirdly, and possibly utmost essential in the communal education area, the educator is a compassionate adviser, an individual who is concerned with the students' overall progression. Educator as designer, facilitator and advisor are merely three of the utmost significant new roles that educators perform, but not all educators must carry out all the roles (Schlechty, 2002). Diverse types of educators with no similar types and stages of preparation and proficiency may concentrate on perhaps choosing one or two of these roles.

3.10 Technology Infrastructure and Ethical Use of Data

Technology infrastructure support is always the most fundamental challenge of all, despite in theory, it is assumed available. Implementation of LA for achieving QA is a journey. Research gap is identified based on different contexts in terms of investigations that cover concerns in the literature review study for the Malaysian and to what extent LA influences the students and teachers' commitment. However, it is still a new technology in education environment in Malaysia. Hence, we seek to identify the difference in effects of analytics among the participant groups according to its curriculum; students' learning outcomes; learning processes; teachers' capacity; and continuous research by following a successful empirically proved theory that was proven in other countries. It is therefore important to investigate this in local context before applying it to the learning and teaching process in HEIs nationwide.

Most important of all is the ethical use of data where a clear understanding must be established across consistently as simple as "what can be done", "what should be done", what must be done" and similarly vice versa (Ferguson & Clow, 2017). Ethics and privacy have become such an alarm as people tend to make profit with the data that they have. As said by Zhou (2018), it is unavoidable as when people have it, people will use it; hence, the legal aspect to manage and the theory beyond technical scope have to be emphasized where we must value the protection. As data collection is continuous, remedial measures to seek solution would be a continuous process like a ripple system.

With reference to the same research done by West et al. (2018) in the preceding paragraphs, the capacity of the institution as a whole with regard to the availability of data sources, its future integration of data and the provision of development are fundamental requirements for the successful adoption of LA by academics. Malaysian academics have a number of challenges, including financial investment in LA, a lack of student data, and a lack of clarity regarding proper PD to guarantee academics are proficient in using LA output reports.

Moreover, Malaysians have very different perceptions regarding the institutions' capacity to meet academics' needs and expectations, which may be related to the developmental stage of LA (West et al., 2018). Again, it is empirically hailed by the researchers that Malaysia is less advanced in LA adoption, and educational information systems are far from integration (West et al., 2018). LA in Malaysia is still at the awareness stage, and the educational data sources are yet to be systematically integrated; hence, academics do not have high expectations regarding LA implementation.

With respect to ethical issues, it is apparent that Malaysian academics express a higher level of concern because of lack of detailed policies to handle learning and teaching data. The ICT policy and e-learning policy that we currently have are very brief and reflect only the needs of the institutional goals (West et al., 2018). As a result, doubts as to what data to collect, for what purpose and how extensive the boundaries are, have become the hurdles to LA application.

3.11 Conclusion

Reviews were done based on the domain of effect on teaching and learning in line with the conceptualization of the framework of study. With the understanding of how knowledge is built, researchers have a better understanding of effective use of data in LA as one of the critical components to increase students' graduate attributes. The nine current issues on students' learning processes and learning outcomes reviewed include rising cost of learning leading to incompletion of programs; learning digital literacy to integrate formal and informal learning approaches; knowledge management; 21st-century skills; transfer of knowledge; response to new methods of teaching and curriculum; response to quality teaching; capacity of teachers for learning reform; and technology infrastructure and ethical use of data.

References

Arroway, P., Morgan, G., O'Keefe, M., & Yanosky, R. (2016). Learning analytics in higher education. *EDUCAUSE*. http://library.educause.edu/~/media/files/library/2016/2/ers1504la.pdf

Avella, J. T., Kebritchi, M., Nunn, S. G., & Kanai, T. (2016). Learning analytics methods, benefits, and challenges in higher education: A systematic literature review. *Online Learning*, *20*(2), 13–29.

Bates, A. W. (2015). Teaching in a digital age – Guidelines for designing teaching and learning. *Creative commons attribution-non-commercial 4.0 international license*. https://bccampus.ca/open-textbook-project/

Biggam, J. (2001). Defining knowledge: An epistemological foundation for knowledge management. *Proceedings of the 34th Hawaii international conference on system sciences*. http://cs.unibo.it/~gaspari/www/teaching/defining_knowledge.pdf

Brown, A. (2011). Online learning: A new paradigm for education. *Journal of Educational Technology*, *32*(1), 12–25.

Campbell, J. P., DeBlois, P. B., & Oblinger, D. G. (2007). Academic analytics: A new tool for a new era. *EDUCASE Review*, *42*(4).

Elmes, J. (2017). *Six significant challenges for technology in higher education in 2017*. https://www.timeshighereducation.com/features/six-significant-challenges-technology-higher-education-2017

Ferguson, R., & Clow, D. (2017). Learning analytics: Avoiding failure. *Educause*. https://er.educause.edu/articles/2017/7/learning-analytics-avoiding-failure

Fischer, G. (2000). Lifelong learning – More than training. Special issue on "Intelligent system/tools in training and life-long learning". *International Journal of Continuing Engineering Education and Life-Long Learning* (Riichiro Mizoguchi & Piet A. M. Kommers, Eds.). http://l3d.cs.colorado.edu/~gerhard/papers/lll99.pdf

Gasevic, D., Dawson, S., & Pardo, A. (2016). How do we start? State and directions of learning analytics adoption. *International council for open and distance education.* http://icde.memberclicks.net/assets/RESOURCES/dragan_la_report%20cc%20licence.pdf

Granados, J. (2015). *The challenges of higher education in the 21st century.* http://www.guninetwork.org/articles/challenges-higher-education-21st-century

Henard, F., & Roseveare, D. (2012). *Fostering quality teaching in higher education: Policies and practices.* http://www.oecd.org/education/imhe/QT%20policies%20and%20practices.pdf

Hofer, B. K., & Pintrich, P. R. (1997). The development of epistemological theories: Belief about knowledge and knowing and the relations to learning. *Review of Educational Research, 67*, 88. https://doi.org/10.3102/00346543067001088

Knight, S., Buckingham Shum, S., & Littleton, K. (2014). Epistemology, assessment, pedagogy: Where learning meets analytics in the middle space. *Journal of Learning Analytics, 1*(2). http://epress.lib.uts.edu.au/journals/index.php/JLA/article/view/3538

Lemos, N. (2007). *An introduction to the theory of knowledge.* Cambridge University Press. http://www.unizar.es/arenas/tc/Lemos,_An_Introduction_to_the_Theory_of_Knowledge_(2007).pdf

Malaysian Qualifications Agency. (2018a). *Code of Practice for Programme Accreditation* (2nd ed.). Retrieved from https://www2.mqa.gov.my/qad/garispanduan/COPPA/2019/Oct/26092019%20CLEAN%20COPPA%202nd%20Edition%20(2017).pdf

Malaysian Qualifications Agency. (2018b). *COPIA form: MQA-03 (Self-Review Portfolio)* (2nd ed.). Retrieved from http://www.mqa.gov.my/portalMQAv3/borang/copia/MQA-03

Miró-Pérez, A. P. (2020). World economic forum: Present and future. *Dimensión Empresarial, 18*(2), 1–7.

Schlechty, P. C. (2002). *Working on the work: An action plan for teachers, principals and superintendents* (1st ed.). Jossey-Bass.

West, D., Luzeckyj, A., Tasir, Z., & Toohey, D. P. (2018). Learning analytics experience among academics in Australia and Malaysia: A comparison. *Australian Journal of Educational Technology, 34*(3), 122–139. https://doi.org/10.14742ajet.3836

Zhou, X. F. (2018). The UQ experience as an analytics driven university. *Panel presentation on "The analytics organization: Challenges and directions" of HELP university annual convocation 21st strategy seminar 2018.* Kuala Lumpur, Malaysia.

Zilvinskis, J., & Boarder, V. (2017). *Learning analytics in higher education. New directions for higher education, 179*(Fall). Jossey-Bass.

4 LA Implementation, Issues, Challenges and the Way Forward

4.1 Introduction

LA is an emergent technology that aims to produce effective learning and learning outcomes, namely knowledge and skills. LA works as follows: utilizes live data accumulated to forecast learner accomplishment, encourages involvement/support established on those predictions and monitors the influence of action. Essentially, the crucial elements involved were clearly data, analysis and actions. Where analytical intelligence is added into the raw data through algorithms, ultimate action would be the goal of the LA process. Data collected from students' interaction in the adaptive learning system are modeled and utilized for pedagogic decision-making to predict students' competence in achieving specific CLO, essentially QA of MQA as a whole. Designing tasks that are valid constitutes operational procedures of skills wherein instructors are trying to model the relevant domain of QA. Early alert system, proactive feedback structure and pre-entry attributes of students are all anticipated in classrooms. Besides LA's implementation, profitable relationships with various stakeholders must be sustained. Leadership to steer the strategic change to institutional culture and conduct is essential.

4.2 Incorporating LA in the Classrooms

As indicated earlier on the issues on students' learning processes and students' learning outcomes, many authoritative organizations have also listed important global issues that humanity is facing, especially with respect to teachers, who are facing complex challenges to help students achieve their full potential for the 21st-century society (UNESCO, 2017). According to Villegas-Remers (2003), technology development is one of the most important and challenging change agent that teachers must embrace, as it necessitates a transformation in pedagogical practices and the integration of innovative tools to enhance student learning outcomes. How can LA be incorporated into classrooms to support educators and learners in an uncertain and complex world?

DOI: 10.4324/9781003584520-4

How do we focus on a method or an approach to predict student accomplishment, and how can those expectations be utilized to notify evidence-informed teaching practices? Thille and Zimmaro (2017) wrote that we should remember that a suitably equipped virtual learning environment allows us to capture information about students' interactions and to use that information to gather commanding response cycles from instructors, learners, as well the program creators and the knowledge of learning.

Looking at how courseware can be planned to concurrently enhance learner learning with the current improvement in neuroscience, intellectual knowledge, computer science and data science for speedy development in the knowledge of human learning for achieving QA in higher education. Nonetheless, the outcomes researchers have in history are not interpreted into fruitful shifts in student learning and instructor teaching (Thille & Zimmaro, 2017). LA incorporating OLI delivers a way for utilizing educational tools to move the connection of learning enquiry and instruction practice in enhancing learner learning. Thille and Zimmaro (2017) wrote that the data that are accumulated from learners' interactions in learning models are structured and utilized for pedagogic decision-making – either the method can spontaneously choose a learning chore for the students or the system will provide instruction to the teacher to predict students' competence in achieving specific CLO and the mapping of CLO with PLO, and certainly, the graduate attributes that conform to QA of the MQA in the case of Malaysia.

Thille and Zimmaro (2017) have also written on creation of opportunities in generating meaning of data. What data? Having given attention to the content of online courses, like content and visualization for prediction of persistence outcomes, what about the measures of students' learning? Other than technological input and data output of online courses, wherein LA frequently concentrated on event and achievement information measures meeting standards of QA, there has not been much capturing on data of learning processes, which may better contain approximations of learning – for instance, the frequency of logging-ins, time consumed on a page and logs for clickstream. de Oliveira et al. (2021) examine how LA can assist in identifying students who are at risk of dropping out of higher education. The research recommends that LA models are able to analyze student data to predict academic performance and potential dropout. This enables educators to intervene early and improve student retention.

The data utilized in the learning process is derived from assessments linked to specific skills and knowledge mechanisms, ensuring alignment with examinations, assignments and evaluations related to the CLO. Additionally, predictions are contingent upon the accuracy of the measurements conducted. It is essential for instructors to design a variety of responsibilities grounded in pertinent philosophies of human learning, as this shapes performance represented by sufficient evidence that can be identified and aggregated to provide a coherent, logical representation of students' knowledge and the learning process (Thille & Zimmaro, 2017).

The planned assessment activity must provide reliable evidence to serve as operational measurements of the skills instructors aim to demonstrate, ensuring relevance to the quality assurance framework. (Thille & Zimmaro, 2017). Besides a division of machine learning, reinforcement learning is a structure that moves the focus of machine learning from a modest form of acknowledgment to an experienced, compelled chronological form in decision-making (Thille and Zimmaro, 2017). Scholars in education and computer science are currently examining the implications of performance-based learning derived from "deep learning" which connects artificial neurons over time. They are exploring how deep learning can enhance our understanding of human knowledge development, and how data generated by thousands of learners across various contexts, when combined with machine learning algorithms, may provide a unique opportunity to discover new methods for learner success. In short, technology-facilitated learning environments continue to progress; for sure, our capability to plan assessment tasks that are more accurate in capturing learner learning will likewise progress.

As for Thille and Zimmaro (2017), the authors of a concern told by the U.S. Department of Education's Office of Education Technology (Bienkowski et al., 2012), they have acknowledged a number of confines in organizational abilities related to gathering/collecting, keeping/storing and sharing data; setup expenses related to hardware, software and human resources; practicability of instrument panels and other information response reports for students and instructors; and possible prejudices in how outcomes are deduced. In short, these are not only institutional-level LA efforts for achieving success in QA but also analytics for the learning process level. The LA system must integrate with other organizational-level data systems to address infrastructure concerns and enhance teaching practices and student learning assistance.LA challenges fundamentally restructure how HEIs reflect on learner accomplishment (Buyarski et al., 2017). It is backed by an example from Indiana University, where LA facilitate student learning, accomplishments and the attainment of goal completion. We should now be able to observe pupil learning. Consequently, we should examine the Malaysian context regarding our perception of student accomplishment. For achieving QA in the Malaysian context, it is essential to ensure that students graduate on time and maintain accountability for their individual learning and achievements. As for Indiana University, the implementation of the LA project is part of the institutionally developed alert system, as noted by Wagner and Longanecker (2016), reflecting technical resourcefulness. The primary institutional framework for student success is supported by constant responses, monitoring, evaluation and communication of learners' achievements through mechanisms such as an early alert system.

Seeing how this system works can further justify LA achieving QA in higher education. According to Faulconer et al. (2014), an early alert system of LA offers a formal, proactive feedback structure through which stakeholders contribute, thereby impacting student performance and, consequently, HEIs. The predictive model evaluates pre-entry characteristics of learners to determine potential threats, aiding in the identification of at-risk students who may face course failure and program incompletion (Cuseo, 2006; Davidson et al., 2009). An early alert system helps address a common concern among students who often do not realize their performance in a subject until it is too late to make any necessary changes. This system also enables higher education institutions (HEIs) to identify and provide support to students who need assistance (Pistilli & Arnold, 2010). What about mid-term grades, of the initial response learners obtain about the course achievement, often arrives excessively late to permit many learners to make any adjustments for improvement whereas LA prompt alert measures provide detailed, behavioral based response and prepare learners with suitable intermediations (Cuseo, 2006; Simmons, 2011).

Overall HEIs with multiple campuses that engage prompt alert arrangements as a technique for improving students' accomplishment report moderate to great contentment with them (Simmons, 2011). To ensure successful implementation, it is essential to adopt LA data as the primary guide for interventions across all departments of HEIs, involving everyone from top leadership to faculty, counselors, and staff who will apply the data to assist learners. (Wagner & Longanecker, 2016). Buyarski et al. (2017) asserted that in order to use LA successfully across institutions, important stakeholders must take part from the start in the plan of the system arrangement. Moreover, vital to the execution of LA are concerns of institutional ability in terms of getting LA implements in the hands of all pertinent people as well as making sure that facilities and backups are accessible to learners with risk issues (Lonn et al., 2012).

4.3 LA and Student Success Intervention

The execution of LA in supporting students' accomplishment needs a workable intervention and usage of feedback data to be tracked and supported, stated Pistilli (2017). In a scenario that Pistilli (2017) used in his paper (Pistilli, 2017, p. 43):

> You are a new faculty member and have been assigned to teach 3 sections of an introductory psychology class. When you receive your course roster, you realize that there are over 200 students, that the department chair has charged you with increasing success rates in the course. As the first assignment and assessment come around, you notice you have a wide range of performance including a large proportion of students earning a C or less. Given that you teach over 600 students and have other requirements as a faculty member, you wonder how you might be able to provide meaningful feedback to students in a data-driven and efficient manner.

Coming back to another definition by the Society of Learning Analytics Research (SoLAR, 2012), LA centers on the measurement, collection, analysis and reporting of data about students and their context with the objective to understand and optimize student learning. This is how HEIs today are turning business intelligence techniques to support student success; here, the final stage of LA is to ascertain risk and decide which interventions are expected to acquire the precise information to the correct learners at the precise time in the correct way so that their achievement advances (Pistilli, 2017). The information presented to students depends on the perspective from which one seeks to determine what should be offered, isn't it? Should students know the grades they have received on their work or works, for instance?

Well, what is the role of feedback and one's academic achievement? Chickering and Gamson (1987) report that frequent feedback is best where learners need to be given a chance to ponder on what they have studied and what they still need to find out, for instance. Indeed, Hattie and Timperley (2007, p. 81) define feedback as "one of the most powerful influences on learning and achievement". Considering the concept of social cognitive theory discussed in the previous section, feedback serves as a vital tool for informing students about the actions they need to take to achieve their Course Learning Outcomes (CLO) (Bandura, 1997). Additionally, learners are motivated by specific outcomes that are deemed essential, which teachers can provide through the use of a learning analytics (LA)-driven intervention.

Providing feedback is important to students' performance; Tanes et al. (2011) reported that extensive feedback is usually ineffective where there is a risk of revealing a little too much details of learners such that they will not go through the message at all. Too much of a good thing may after all not be effective; instead, as Clow (2012) states, it is also imperative to inspect intermediary efforts like intervention, not just to evaluate the consequences of our doing.

In an LA cycle, presented by Clow (2012), which has four linked steps from learner to data to metrics and intervention, learners generate data, which is used to generate metrics, analytics and visualization in order to make interventions that influence learners. According to Clow (2012), the LA cycle is a feedback loop where the four stakeholders are learners (i.e., the central agent of the loop), the teachers (i.e., the individual who is involved personally in the process), managers and policy makers (who are responsible for organizational administration and policies setting). In this case, learner benefits from personalized information that teachers operate on the basis of their knowledge, which includes all profession-related insights that affect the teaching and learning situation. Heilala (2018) in her master's thesis of mathematical information technology applied the cyclical process of Clow (2012) to pedagogical LA which results is pedagogical LA makes use of educational knowledge discovery process in order to provide valid, novel and useful knowledge which teachers can utilize when creating and optimizing teaching – learning situation and environment across subjects. Well, although pedagogical LA is a tool for practitioners, the concept has to be grounded on the theory of learning. Future further empirical research is needed to prove the effectiveness of pedagogical LA in that part.

Of the implementations utilizing varied methodologies using numerous objects, as per Gasevic et al. (2016), there are three main themes in LA execution or implementation: that is, the progress of the predictor and pointers for numerous elements such as academic performance, learners' commitment and engagement, and personalized-planned learning skills; the visualization to discover and construe information and to trigger corrective steps; and, finally, the descent of mediations to form the learning surroundings. It is a complex process, wherein this diversity always poses a challenge for HEIs to common voices of "How do we start the process for the adoption of institutional LA?" and "To what extent LA can predict and thus achieve the QA in this case?"

Berry (2017) found that age, educational level, academic capacity, the period of registration and prime major college are prognostic of stranger academic accomplishment regardless of the program layout. Well, there is very minimum research done on how LA achieves QA in higher education; however, the above-mentioned can be used as a guideline.

4.4 Cultivating Institutional Capacity of Key Stakeholders for LA

HEIs' key objective of presence is to create and distribute knowledge for the improvement of practically all aspects of life. Thus, it is understood who matters in the HEIs, and the ability to look at HEIs in Malaysia is vital. Success of using LA for academic achievements of students as well as institutions is hence based on the amount of actions reinforced by main stakeholders, which comprise heads of faculty, students, IT infrastructure, community and financial supports (Lonn et al., 2017).

As HEIs are undergoing a process of transformation, its function is being reassessed in particular to emphasize the input they can create to the well-being of their economic and societal surroundings (Mainardes et al., 2010). Thus, HEIs must be involved in a money-making relationship with different stakeholders, and before that, they must ascertain those stakeholders and their desires before outlining urgencies and related approaches for individual entity. The identification and classification of stakeholders are indeed prerequisites for the development of operations and improvement of quality in stakeholder relationships (Kettunen, 2015). As a whole, effective implementation of LA entails a leader to steer important and strategic shifts to institutional culture and behavior (Baepler & Murdoch, 2010; Norris et al., 2009).

Wong (2017) emphasized the benefits of LA for the stakeholders revolve around aspects as follows: to reduce the students' attrition rate if more accurate, if not precise data can be traced, including learners' learning diligence, unwanted learning behavior and emotive dispositions, all to be identified with the prediction models, upon which implementation can be supported by extra counseling rapidly with the suggested learning resources and individual learning plan that indirectly contribute to QA. Besides, response on students' development and progress could be delivered to learners and lecturers more cost-effectively as LA can be integrated with the respective LMS (Wong, 2017). In these aspects, resource allocation can be optimized, communication among all stakeholders can be enhanced, and better evaluation on pedagogies and teaching strategies for quality improvement and assurance for better QA is commonly measured by various gauges such as Grade Point Average, learning development, retention and graduation ratio. Bujang et al. (2021) explore using predictive analytics to improve student success in higher education. The authors developed a model using previous students' academic results from 489 Information and Communication Technology students to predict final grades. Comparison of data was used by four machine-learning methods, and it was found that a decision tree model achieved the highest accuracy (nearly 99.6%). This model could help educators to identify students who are at risk of dropping out. In that case, the school can take early action to improve their chances of success.

However, his research identified that where LA is a new capacity in HEIs, there still exist lots of qualms, especially for the non-conventional face-to-face education such as online learning. Also, it is a challenge identified by Wong (2017) in assessing the efficacy of LA application where it is difficult to identify to the degree to which any adjustment after the LA implementation is accredited to the LA itself. In measuring the effectiveness of LA implementation according to Sclater and Mullan (2017), it may not be useful to isolate the influence of LA when it is part of a broader benefit to mend data-based procedures in an organization. Hence, for the answer in this case to "To what extent QA is achieved upon implementation of LA?", it is yet to be known.

As mentioned earlier in previous section, Clow (2012) has indicated in his LA cycle theory that four stakeholders are in a feedback loop. The extent to which learners benefit from personalized information provided by teachers—who draw on their professional insights that influence the teaching and learning environment—needs further exploration in future research. This investigation should examine the roles and contributions of each stakeholder involved, aiming to uncover new insights into student learning and to foster a culture of continuous improvement in higher education institutions (HEIs) regarding the learning and teaching process.

4.5 Ethical Use of Data in LA

Can LA be implemented ethically? There are lots of intricate challenges to be overcome on the concerns on privacy, even to less well-assumed apprehensions with the system in perspective within the framework of information, operation and institutional configurations influencing capabilities for self-growth and willpower (Johnson, 2017). In this context, we are certainly looking at the notion of LA and academic analytics in the later stage both interconnected in achieving QA in higher education. As wrote by Johnson

(2017) in his paper "Ethics and Justice in Learning Analytics", we take a look at four ethical questions in LA, namely privacy, individuality, autonomy and discrimination.

Besides, Hoel et al. (2017) also commented on the fact that there is a gap between the concerns and obstacles of implementing LA ethically. LA opens up an intricate setting of confidentiality and strategy matters, which, in turn, impact how LA systems and practices are planned (Hoel et al., 2017). Certainly, research and expansion are administered by code of practice for storing information and managing it and by research integrities. Subsequently, when stirring clarifications out of the research laboratories, executors encounter restraints defined in nationwide regulations and warranted in discretion charters. To what extent do OECD, APEC and EU confidentiality charters search to control data confidentiality which in turn impacts significantly on the discourse of LA in Malaysia, including the influence on tools' design, planning and practices?

A thorough list of necessities for LA systems needs to be established centered on the new lawful demands explained in the European General Data Protection Regulation (GDPR); this will be imposed as European law from 2018, which possibly impacts the diverse confidentiality charters on the design of LA privacy solutions on the usage of educational data (Hoel et al., 2017) – in this case Malaysia. For instance, in the seminar paper presented by Hoel and Chen (2016), it is to a great extent to the amount of personal data, the extent of processing of their storage and accessibility are to be measured and to meet the privacy requirements and obligations of the GDPR.

Privacy refers to relations of data streams (Nissenbaum, 2010) where privacy privileges are sheltered by averting data to those that do not have the legitimate right to such information. The question is when the flow of information and privacy where LA combines institution data for analysis for building predictive models where it is used to predict student outcomes. Of the information such as class attendance, self-restraint and incapacity, it could be perceived as interfering, though it is a narrow interpretation; the extent to which consent is an essential feature should be taken into consideration as privacy violations, especially information flow from a campus to another campus. "The recognition of student individuality is also problematic in LA", wrote Johnson (2017). The issue is that LA does not act on human beings instead cerates being composed bulks of data to correspond with human beings. As said, the dehumanization is then enforced on the learners as institutional resolutions are achieved centered not on humanistic complexities of a person and societal connotation by machine-driven procedures of qualifying, grouping and responding. For instance, a decision tree model utilized by one institution to forecast retention by GPA may not be the case of another unique case as no one characteristic is distinct.

More often than not, systems operate more paternalistically than one believes to think critically and can act further for their own good. Can you imagine the system reflected learner actions in earlier classes and suggested classes that would get the best out of learners' GPA and thus chances of retaining scholarship and completing their studies? It nonetheless severely constraints student autonomy within the framework of disciplinary power (Parry, 2011). One growing concern among numerous others in big data most common is its potential for "algorithmic discrimination", in the notion of social norms underlying analytics processes (Johnson, 2017). Many research studies have been laid; however, none has said that LA is inherently unethical, wrote Johnson (2017). Rather ensuring firstly that LA is not merely value-unbiased calculation established on impartial data and second that a just LA is not only on the issue of good faith, administers are confronted with inevitable ethical queries. LA is not being criticized here instead it is being argued for an overall sanction against the field, and that is the case here.

Johnson (2017) has indeed highlighted five factors to strengthen and legalize social hierarchy of the use of LA for its purposes, namely the true intent of interest in LA, broad negotiated process, transparent problem-model-intervention, valid representation of data; and lastly, logical model which connects problems and intervention. Good research questions can be grounded in the future based on the mentioned careful attention indeed.

4.6 Issues, Challenges and the Way Forward

LA is an emergent technological practice and a multidisciplinary scientific discipline whose ultimate goal is to produce effective learning and its outcome. Despite recent efforts as mentioned earlier, LA has not yet fully managed to redeem its promises (Ferguson & Clow, 2017). Having analyzed benefits of LA and its promises, what are the management challenges to be overcome, including LA imperatives to policy challenges? As identified by Macfadyen et al. (2014), there are needs for a change in the belief, framework in technology, instructional practices in HEIs, from "assessment for accountability to assessment for learning" which cannot be attained through fragmentary execution of a new tool. As HEIs are an example of a highly complex adaptive system, we are arriving into an era in which learning may take place anyway, at any moment using different kinds of devices via multiple kinds of interaction. Will a new form of leadership, collaboration, policy development or strategic planning emerge for optimizing the education system toward QA?

4.6.1 Strategic Direction and Change

According to the guest blog by Pineda Lindsay published by Scalter (2017), trends observed in organizational level on LA include culture, process and communication. Pineda Lindsay wrote that there are notable challenges regarding the level of comfort and willingness to accept changes to current practices relating to job roles or additional responsibilities; significant variances in the understanding of what would be required in terms of level of effort among leadership members; and tones of resistance experienced from academics who have prescriptive allocation of their time related to teaching and advising.

Also, as we learned that a clear and non-overarching conceptualization of the benefits that LA has toward improving QA in higher education is fundamental, resistance to change and adaptability of the stakeholders toward LA also play a critical role in establishing a positive relationship. Rick (2013) also wrote that foreseeing defiance to adjustment and preparing for it from the beginning of the change management will permit educators to reduce doubts of the stakeholders. There are eight most shared beliefs and causes for people to repel transformation according to Rick (2013), that is to say there isn't any actual need for the transformation; the transformation will make it harder for them to reach their needs; the threats seem to be greater than the advantages; they don't they have the capability to realize the transformation; they believe the transformation will be unsuccessful; transformation procedure is being handled inappropriately by administration; the transformation is not aligned with their beliefs; they are certain that those in control for the transformation can't be trusted.

Lewin's model, as discussed by Hussain et al. (2016), was utilized for institutional transformation process where leadership plays an important role in unfreezing the organization in which transformational leadership flair coordinate with member of staff, partake their knowledge, and provide a chance in creating resolutions in institutional level, and the positive relationship integrates employees and leaders into one unit. Furthermore, framework makes available a vision to general practitioner that just how leaders' actions related to participation and partaking knowledge in the process of change (Hussain et al., 2016). Hence, change factor is crucial for the institution to transform into believing in and adopting the tool of LA and its benefits to the students, staffs and other stakeholders. In reflecting it to the system of current education system, unfreezing is thus necessary when the change is planned. In addition, stakeholders' adaptability toward the new reality of how profoundly digital technologies have impacted the key domain of education is critical.

In this case, Ployhart and Bliese in year 2006 wrote that adaptableness denotes a person's capability, skill, nature, readiness and/or motivation to impulse to transform or apt diverse duty, societal or ecological types (Zhou & Lin, 2016). Zhou and Lin (2016) also wrote that flexibility/adaptability is considered to be an important fundamental foundation of psychological resources. To adapt to shifting state of affairs, Ployhart and Bliese in year 2006 wrote that one has to display flexibility both in cognizance and actions (Zhou & Lin, 2016). Hence, overcoming management challenges, a useful strategy to create pleasure and success through improving quality of life via high performance in competencies in the 21st century, is thus significant. For instance, as far as organizational support for LA is concerned, staff were quite concerned with the impact of their current job requirement; hence, a "top-down" directive from leadership members would be necessary to properly implement LA efforts.

As in infrastructure according to Scalter (2017), most institutions did not have the organizational infrastructure at present to support the implementation and adoption of LA. Have we had a formalized structure or did we know what other departmental staff did daily which affects each other? Hence, issues about redundancy, additional workload and time management are critical management challenges.

4.6.2 Leadership and Culture

Today, educational leadership has improved significantly where it has contributed very much to students' achievement (Kapur, 2018). It is typically the duty of the school superintendents and heads or department chair and academic dean who struggle to generate affirmative transformation in educational guiding principle and procedures, to improve learning system, to lead new directions and guide their policies and practices and to carry out their work effectually? Moreover, globalization is also a fashionable theoretical stance today in education where leadership at local-global axis needs to be paid more attention, especially on trends in new managerialism, academic capitalism and entrepreneurial universities (Deem, 2010).

What is the philosophy underlays leadership in education, which in this the job duties of the educational leaders are more focused upon in the change process? It depends on the frontrunners to implement the responsibilities and purposes in a proper fashion to attain the sought-after aims and objectives of the educational organization (Kapur, 2018). In Kapur's (2018) study, she wrote that leading to the empowerment of other individuals to create important resolutions has always been considered as the principal aim of leaders while other goals include giving teaching assistance, creating and executing planned and school improvement plans, developing teacher quality, improving in teaching and learning processes, and reforming and improving the program of study. As cited by Robinson (2007) from Cambridge Assessment International Education in 2015, "The more leaders focus their professional relationships, their work and their learning on the core business of teaching and learning, the greater the influence on student outcomes" (p. 12).

The diversity of views about leadership is based on the perspectives of educational leadership such as instructional leadership, transformational leadership, moral leadership, participative leadership, managerial leadership and contingency leadership (Cambridge Assessment International Education, 2015; Kapur, 2018). Summary of the diversity views is summarized in Table 4.1.

Table 4.1 Perspectives of Educational Leadership

Perspectives	*Concepts*
Instructional leadership	Focuses on school's core business such as teaching and learning.
Transformational leadership	Concerned with commitment of colleagues, leading change and improving performance.
Moral leadership	Emphasizes the importance of values, vision and ethical leadership.
Participative leadership	Stresses the importance of including colleagues, sharing decision-making and social capital.
Managerial leadership	Stresses the importance of defining functions, tasks and behaviors.
Contingency leadership	Highlights how leaders respond to the particular organizational circumstances and challenges they face and encounter over time.

Source: Adapted from Cambridge Assessment International Education, 2015; Kapur, 2018

Globalization has indeed triggered a need for leaders with better comprehension of cultural variance and greater-than-before proficiencies in cross-cultural communication and norms. According to Northhouse (2013), scholars acknowledged that worldwide leadership characteristics can be utilized to illustrate how diverse cultural clusters understand leadership, namely value-based, team-oriented participation and humanitarian-oriented, self-directed, self-defending leadership. Leadership fundamentally underpins principles and standards, with the primary concern for leaders being the comprehension of the intricate layers of culture and the management of the apprehensions that arise, subsequently confronting those expectations. Linking to realism and facts, all categories of social order are established on in-depth expectations on common abstract concerns. Isn't this how individuals relate to reality and facts, how individuals should relate to one another? Getting agreement for example challenges how well the group of people is led to build a shared social reality in a university.

With regard to policy management, either institutions have it or they do not currently have it, there were great discrepancies in most institutions regarding how the staff and leadership perceived the management of policies and practices. As a result, issues of micromanagement, current inconsistencies, the execution of their accountability and whether LA would add to their already-overloaded requirements. As much as the issue of the ease of integration with existing organizational structure, according to Scalter (2017), many institutions liked the theory and ideas behind it; however, they were uncertain on how it would actually be implemented. And, the question of how to determine who would be responsible for implementation was a topic of debate, especially when the use of lecturers/tutors is divided.

Discussion on the theoretical problems of the study is always the most significant part of the research. Besides the notion of culture with respect to resistance to change and adaptability, strategic direction is utmost important as leadership will be the backbone of technology infrastructure. Additionally, a teacher's ability to recognize how different pedagogical approaches influence their teaching practices allows them to identify which algorithms and visualizations could be educationally beneficial. This understanding can lead to the redefinition and redevelopment of new policies. Norris et al. (2008) also wrote that, due to the growing responsibility demand and presence escalation in performance evaluation, HEIs' leaders often search for to instill as much as into the intricate decision-making procedures that include the preparation of planning and process/operations of the HEIs and programs.

Of that notion, deployment of LA projects through a substantial number of strategies (even simultaneously) is indeed crucial, upon which policies are to be laid in more detailed themes. Incorporation of broad vision of academic excellence, good judgment of investment potential and the full engagement of faculties are three main themes emerged in recent years (Zilvinskis et al., 2017). In this context, Zilvinskis and Boarder (2017) emphasize that higher education institutions (HEIs) are complex organizations that require support not only from academics but also from staff leaders, management, and students. All stakeholders must have a clear understanding of the problems they are trying to address, the gradual steps needed to resolve these issues, and who can assist in the process. As concluded by West et al. (2018), besides technology being an important consideration, human factors, especially the integrated culture in using data and analytics by all LA stakeholders, are paramount to the success of implementation and hence the determinant factors for the long-term use of LA.

According to the Malaysia Higher Education Blueprint (Ministry of Higher Education, 2015–2025) in a broader perspective, the Ministry's paramount desire is to generate a higher education scheme/structure that is rated among the globe's paramount systems of education and that allows Malaysia to contest in the worldwide economy. Specifically, the Ministry aspires to produce graduates with a determination to generate employments rather than merely hunt for employments and to balance citizens with entrepreneurial mindset; educational paths that emphasizes an equivalent importance on much desirable technical and vocational preparation; concentration on results over inputs through pursuing technologies and innovations for better personalization of learning involvements as well as experience (transformed HEIs delivery); coordination in regulating private and public institutions for autonomy within the regulatory framework; and all stakeholders to have collective obligations for resources in higher education as to make certain that higher education financial factor can be sustained. As the envisioned 11-year transformation of the higher education system is comprehensive and multifaceted, while the Government and the Ministry are dedicated fresh approaches of doing things so as to provide noteworthy, justifiable and extensive outcomes as well as keeping leadership pledge and emphases as the number one priority, HEIs are ready to be culturally led to make this a reality? Outcome will be drawn in the findings later in this report.

4.7 Conclusion

The review focused on interventions designed to deliver precise information to the right students at the appropriate time and in the most effective manner, with the aim of improving their performance. Through feedback which is the greatest authoritative impact on learning and achievement, it is not just assessment of outcome of our action but also examination of immediate effort like intervention. It was discussed whether age, education level, academic load and the term of enrollment were predictive of academic performance. Lastly, can LA be done ethically? Issues on privacy, individuality, autonomy and discrimination were discussed, including solidifying and legitimating the LA process.

Moreover, values include boosting retention rate (identifying struggling students earlier); performance tracking to increase learning success rate; adjustment of students' own path and pace of learning; types of learning-tailored instruction; and real-time feedback. Besides, it is a platform to continuously upskill the academics and enhance educational research. Well, the focus of instructors and institutional concerns is different. LA will only benefit if it is implemented correctly with full participation of all required stakeholders. Implementation challenges such as the value of LA and its embeddedness for success in the context of students, faculty and management. Challenges in strategic direction and change, and leadership and culture were discussed (Gasevic et al. 2016; Scalter 2017).

References

Badura, A. (1997). Self-efficacy: Towards a unifying theory of behavior change. *Psychological Review*, *84*(2), 191–215.

Baepler, P., & Murdoch, C. J. (2010). Academic analytics and data mining in the higher education. *International Journal for Scholarship of Teaching and Learning*, *4*(2), 1–9. https://doi.org/10.20429/ijsotl.2010.040217

Berry, L. J. (2017). *Using learning analytics to predict academic success in online and face-to-face learning environment.* https://scholarworks.boisestate.edu/cgi/viewcontent.cgi?article=2317&context=td#page64

Bienkowski, M., Feng, M. Y., & Means, B. (2012). *U.S. Department of Education. Enhancing teaching and learning through educational data mining and learning analytics: An issue brief.* https://tech.ed.gov/wp-content/uploads/2014/03/edm-la-brief.pdf

Bujang, S. D. A., Selamat, A., & Krejcar, O. (2021). A predictive analytics model for students' grade prediction by supervised machine learning. In

IOP conference series: Materials science and engineering (Vol. 1051, No. 1, p. 012002). IOP Publishing.

Buyarski, C., Murray, J., & Torstrick, R. (2017). Learning analytics across a statewide system. In J. Zilvinskis & V. Boarder (Eds.), *Learning analytics in higher education. New directions for higher education, 179* (Fall). Jossey-Bass.

Chickering, A. W., & GAmson, Z. F. (1987). Seven principles for good practice in undergraduate education. *AAHE Bulletin, 39*(7), 3–7.

Clow, D. (2012). The learning analytics cycle: Closing the loop. In D. Gasevic & S. Buckingham Shum (Eds.), *Proceedings from the 2nd International Learning Analytics and knowledge conference* (p. 1340138). ACM. http://doi.org/10.1145/2330601.2330636

Cuseo, J. (2006). *Behavioral indicators of potential student attrition.* http://www.uwc.edu/sites/uwc.edu/files/imce-uploads/employees/academic-resources/esfy/_files/red_flags-behavioral_indicators_of_potential_student_attrition.pdf

Cuseo, J. B. (2006). *The empirical case for the importance of first-year seminars: A review of the literature*. In *First-Year Experience and Students in Transition* (pp. 1–15).

de Oliveira, C. F., et al. (2021). How does learning analytics contribute to prevent students' dropout in higher education: A systematic literature review. *Big Data and Cognitive Computing, 5*(4), 64.

Deem, R. (2010). Globalization, new managerialism, academic capitalism and entrepreneurialism in universities: Is the local dimension still important? *On Comparative Education.* http://tandfonline.com

Faulconer, J., Geissler, J., Majewski, D., & Trifilo, J. (2014). Adoption of an early-alert system to support university student success. *Delta Kappa Gamma Bulletin, 80*(2), 45–48.

Ferguson, R., & Clow, D. (2017). Learning analytics: Avoiding failure. *Educause*. https://er.educause.edu/articles/2017/7/learning-analytics-avoiding-failure

Gasevic, D., Dawson, S., & Pardo, A. (2016). How do we start? State and directions of learning analytics adoption. *International council for open and distance education.* http://icde.memberclicks.net/assets/RESOURCES/dragan_la_report%20cc%20licence.pdf

Hattie, J., & Timperley, H. (2007). The power of feedback. *Review of Educational Research, 77*(1), 81–112.

Heilala, V. (2018). *Framework for pedagogical learning analytics*. https://pdfs.semanticscholar.org/6501/48db45822aacf80313ae57208684ebad3b08.pdf

Hoel, T., & Chen, W. (2016). Privacy-driven design of learning analytics applications–exploring the design space of solutions for data sharing and interoperability. *Journal of Learning Analytics, 3*(1), 139–158.

Hoel, T., Griffiths, D., & Chen, W. (2017). The influence of data protection and privacy frameworks on the design of learning analytics system. *LAK. Proceedings of the seventh international learning analytics & knowledge conference* (pp. 243–252). https://doi.org/10.1145/3027385.3027414

Hussain, S. T., Lei, S., Akram, M. J., Hussain, S. H., & Ali, M. (2016). Kurt Lewin's change model. Critical review of the role of leadership and employee involvement in organizational change. *Journal of Innovation & Knowledge (JIK)*, *3*(3), 123–127. https://www.econstor.eu/handle/10419/190739

Johnson, J. A. (2017). Ethics and justice in learning analytics. In J. Zilvinskis & V. Boarder (Eds.), *Learning analytics in higher education. New directions for higher education, 179* (Fall) (pp. 77–87). Jossey-Bass.

Kapur, R. (2018). Educational leadership. *ResearchGate*. https://www.researchgate.net/publication/323691649_Educational_Leadership

Kettunen, J. (2015). Stakeholder relationships in higher education. *Tertiary Education and Management, 21*(1), 56065. https://doi.org/10.1080/13583883.2014.997277

Lonn, S., Krumm, A. E., Waddington, R. J., & Teasley, S. D. (2012). Bridging the gap from knowledge to action: Putting analytics in the hands of academic advisors. *LAK'12 proceedings of the 2nd international conference on learning analytics and knowledge*. New York.

Lonn, S., McKay, T. A., & Teasley, S. D. (2017). Cultivating institutional capacities for learning analytics. In J. Zilvinskis & V. Boarder (Eds.), *Learning analytics in higher education. New directions for higher education, 179* (Fall). Jossey-Bass.

Macfadyen, L. P., Awson, S., Pardo, A., & Gasevic, D. (2014). Embracing big data in complex educational system: The learning analytics imperative and policy challenge. *Research & Practice in Assessment*, *9*(4), 17–28. http://www.rpajournal.com/dev/wp-content/uploads/2014/10/A2.pdf

Mainardes, E. W., Alves, H., & Raposo, M. (2010). An exploratory research on the stakeholders of a university. *Journal of Management and Strategy*, *1*(1). https://doi.org/10.5430/jms.v1n1p76

Ministry of Higher Education. (2015). *Malaysia education blueprint 2015–2025 (higher education)* (Malaysia, Ministry of Higher Education, Putrajaya). Ministry of Higher Education. https://www.um.edu.my/docs/default-source/about-um_document/media-centre/um-magazine/4-executive-summary-pppm-2015-2025.pdf?sfvrsn=

Nissenbaum, H. (2010). *Privacy in context: Technology, policy, and the integrity of social life*. Stanford Law Books.

Norris, D., Baer, L., & Offerman, M. (2009, September 23–29). A national agenda for action analytics. *National symposium of action analytics*. http://lindabaer.efoliomn.com/Uploads/SettingaNationalAgendaforActionAnalytics101509.pdf

Norris, D., Baer, L., Leonard, J., Pugliese, L., & Lefrere, P. (2008). Action analytics measuring and improving performance that matters in higher education. *EDUCAUSE Review*, *43*(1) (January/February 2008), 42–67. https://er.educause.edu/~/media/files/article-downloads/erm0813.pdf

Northouse, P. G. (2013). *Leadership: Theory and Practice* (6th ed.). Thousand Oaks, CA: SAGE Publications.

Parry, M. (2011). College mine data to tailor students' experience. *The chronicle of higher education*. http://chronicle.com/article/A-Moneyball-Approach-to/130062/

Pistilli, M. D. (2017). The role of learning analytics in higher education: A review of the literature. *Journal of Learning Analytics*, *4*(1), 1–20. https://doi.org/10.18608/jla.2017.41.1

Pistilli, M. D., & Arnold, K. E. (2010). Purdue signals: Mining real-time academic data to enhance student success. *About Campus*, *15*(3), 22–24. Thousand Oaks California.

Rick, T. (2013). *Resistant to change is a problem*. https://www.torbenrick.eu/blog/change-management/change-is-not-the-problem-resistance-to-change-is-the-problem/

Robinson, V. (2007). School leadership and student outcomes: Identifying what works and why. *Australia: ACEL Monograph Series*, *41*.

Scalter, N. (2017). Learning analytics adoption and implementation plan. *Effective learning analytic*. https://analytics.jiscinvolve.org/wp/2017/03/21/learning-analytics-adoption-and-implementation-trends

Sclater, N., & Mullan, J. (2017). *Jisc briefing: Learning analytics and student success – assessing the evidence*. https://repository.jisc.ac.uk/6560/1/learning-analytics_and_student_success.pdf

Simmons, J. M. (2011). *A national study of student early alert models at four-year institutions of higher education* [Doctoral dissertation]. ProQuest Dissertations and Thesis database (UMI 3482551).

SoLAR (Society for Learning Analytics Research). (2012). http://www.solareserch.org/about/

Tanes, Z., Arnold, K., Selzer King, A., & Remnet, M. A. (2011). Using signals for appropriate feedback: Perceptions and practices. *Computers & Education*, *57*, 2414–2422.

Thille, C., & Zimmaro, D. (2017). Incorporating learning analytics in the classroom. In J. Zilvinskis & V. Boarder (Eds.), *Learning analytics in higher education. New directions for higher education, 179* (Fall). Jossey-Bass.

UNESCO. (2017). *Unpacking sustainable development goal 4: Education 2030*. https://unesdoc.unesco.org/ark:/48223/pf0000246300

Wagner, E., & Longajecker, D. (2016). Scaling student success with predictive analytics: Reflections after four years in the data trenches. *Change*, *48*(1), 52–58.

West, D., Luzeckyj, A., Tasir, Z., & Toohey, D. P. (2018). Learning analytics experience among academics in Australia and Malaysia: A comparison. *Australian Journal of Educational Technology*, *34*(3), 122–139. https://doi.org/10.14742ajet.3836

Wong, T. M. B. (2017). Learning analytics in higher education: Analysis in case studies. *Asia Association of Open Universities Journal*, *12*(1), 21–40. https://doi.org/10.1108/AAOUJ-01-2017-0009

Zhou, M., & Lin, W. (2016). Adaptability and life satisfaction: The moderating role of social support. *Frontiers in Psychology*, *7*(1134). https://doi.org/10.3389/fpsyg.2016.01134. https://www.ncbi.nlm.nih.gov/pmc/articles/PMC4963457/

Zilvinskis, J., & Boarder, V. (2017). *Learning analytics in higher education. New directions for higher education, 179* (Fall). Jossey-Bass.

5 QA in Higher Education

5.1 Academic Quality Assurance

Apprehensions about value of higher education are never new; however, they have been an inherent fragment of any argument on the issue. Over the years, various advancements have occurred in the assessment, monitoring and enhancement of teaching and learning components, particularly in ideas such as "quality assurance," which are extensively utilized nowadays within the broader procedures of handling quality excellence (Pavel, 2012). Quality indeed is at the highest of utmost agendas, and quality improvement or QA is possibly the most imperative mission faced by HEIs (Sallis, 2002).

So, what is "quality"? There are a few prominent authors on quality like Edwards Deming, Joseph Juran and Philip B Crosby; however, quality is "Fitness for purpose," according to Joseph Juran (Sallis, 2002). What is "assurance" then? It is "conformance to requirements," according to Philip Crosby. Hence, QA in education is an ongoing process to ensure that the agreed standard is delivered, including the ability to potentially achieve high quality of outcome. According to ESIB (2002), QA is the mechanism by which an institution ensures the maintenance and enhancement of the standards and quality of its educational offerings with assurance and precision. According to Mok (2011), QA may also be defined as the systematic administration and evaluation practices and measures adopted by HEIs to ensure the attainment of established benchmarks. Their contribution to the quality initiative has been outstanding. Isn't it challenging to assess educational quality without including their perspectives? In this instance, the QA of HEIs is evaluated according to the QA system of MQA in Malaysia. In the context of globalization and internationalization, institutional diversity is to be matched not only with the QA system of the country but also across national borders to certain extent; transformation is associated rectifying the past, social and economic disparities in cultures and commerce and most importantly the environment of teaching and learning (Chinomona, 2013). The process of transition involves recognizing that the previous command is inadequate for current demands, while the new landscape supplants or complements the older order. This pertains to an innovative method of accomplishment, new insights and a novel technique to addressing societal necessities for existence.

DOI: 10.4324/9781003584520-5

The concept of student-centered learning has emerged as a result of OBET, leading to the increasing replacement of traditional lectures with approaches such as active learning, immersive learning, self-directed learning, or autonomous learning (Pillay, 2002). So, what does it imply? In the framework of learning and teaching, as QA is the systematic measurement monitoring processes and performance, isn't this meeting the principles of Juran's "fitness for purpose," where the product is education in this case, and Crosby's "Conformance to requirement" means mistakes should be minimized? To relate this to the purpose of education, Aristotle stated in *Book VIII* of politics that "this education and these studies exist for their own sake" (ESIB, 2002). In this perspective, hence, QA must occur side by side to back the principle of "fitness for the purpose" of education, where it should fulfill its role in ensuring that students acquire fundamental 21st-century competencies to become responsible citizens and engage in lifelong learning. Consequently, QA is the responsibility of all individuals in higher education. Brennan and Shah (2000) asserted that the importance of QA parallels academic standards, which involve monitoring students' learning progress in alignment with their learning outcomes in real time, in accordance with higher education policies that fulfill the requisite knowledge and skills acquisition of a program. The enhancement of the quality of HEIs is a perpetual endeavor; therefore, the constant development of quality is the focal point of the study. In this instance, QA is examined at the institutional level, focusing on the outcomes of LA about the quality, standards, and significance of services in HEIs, particularly within the context of these specific case studies. The effective utilization of learning analytics is empirically a vital element of a digital learning strategy aimed at personalizing instruction for a greater number of students, particularly to enhance their results at the tertiary level.

As defined by the British Standards Institution (1991), "quality is a totality of features and characteristics of a product/services that bear on its ability to satisfy stated or implied needs" (p. 7). A standard is defined as the documented declaration of selected educational outcomes and their associated evaluation criteria concerning the quality of anticipated achievements; furthermore, applicability refers to the relevance of the instruction in addressing the future needs of the students. Researchers must recognize that quality in higher education, particularly in today's knowledge-based society, is a multifaceted and dynamic concept, intricately connected to the contextual circumstances of an educational framework and the organizational objectives, especially within private HEIs in specific systems and disciplines (Pavel, 2012). Hence, according to Pavel (2012), quality may produce varied, occasionally conflicting interpretations based on the understanding of the divergent interests of various stakeholders. This is influenced by the context in which the input, process and output are evaluated, the characteristics of the academic realm that merit examination and the historical context of the evolution of higher education in the country. There has consistently been a societal imperative to elevate and enhance the quality of existence, encompassing the caliber of pupils' education, the methods of their learning, and their motivations for learning. Consequently, QA involves integrating quality into processes to ensure that the product is developed according to specified requirements (Sallis, 2002). It merely means that QA is a way of generating defect- and fault-free products. Where the goal according to Crosby is "zero defect", QA is thus about constantly fulfilling product requirement or doing things correct first time and each time (Sallis, 2002). This is where the QA system is laid down to assure that the quality of goods or services is assured where a system is engaged (Sallis, 2002).

5.2 QA of Higher Education in Malaysia

Sallis (2002) in his research also led him to the decision that education organizations are going for quality enhancement for several significant causes. Some associate it with ethical and professional obligations, while others perceive it as competitiveness in the marketplace or the demand to demonstrate accountability in a commercial context. Sallis (2002) argues that the imperative for existence drives quality enhancement; however, the complexity of education and the significance of values justify the need for a more nuanced and diverse approach to quality perspectives. Learning constitutes a fundamental aspect of education (Sallis, 2002); if QA is to guarantee relevance in education, it must emphasize the quality of the learner's familiarity and experience, which is the focus of this research study.

To be able to entice worldwide students to Malaysia, the government recognizes the significance of classifying or branding Malaysian education. Susan (2008) narrates that the Malaysian branding in education induces on deep cultural, brand draws on deep cultural, religious and political qualities to endorse its programs, the system that give emphasis to way of life, culture and education quality. As elaborated by Susan (2008), Malaysia exhibits an extraordinary level of flexibility in the globalization of the higher education market. Hence, to ensure HEIs are more competitive, besides adopting strategies to initiate new market in Malaysia, initiatives to utilize intelligence are crucial to make Malaysian brand more unique and attractive. Certainly, one of the issues is that QA looks closely for a healthy and sustainable growth. Back then in 2005, the cabinet has achieved a key resolution to form MQA, which is held accountable for excellent assurance in higher education and to carry out the MQF. Due to the rapid expansion of the higher education structure, QA has developed an operational device for expert acknowledgment of HEIs in Malaysia. The formation of MQA, with its COPPA and COPIA as well as its SETARA, MyQuest and MyRA, is thus crucial to safeguard that HEIs deliver pertinent excellent education to learners. Upholding the government's hope to make Malaysia an "education hub" by 2020 is thus significant to advance the Malaysian higher education structure and system to new pinnacles.

The effort of the MQA circles around two key approaches to QA in higher education in Malaysia (MQA, 2018a). As per the COPPA (MQA, 2018a), the initial approach is to endorse courses and programs and qualification, whereas the following is to appraise and check the organizations on their modules. With that, numerous methodologies to QA practices would normally consist of intermittent supervision to safeguard that value is sustained and constantly enriched and to ensure relevance and currency. MQA over time thus will develop new program standards and guidelines to cover the entire array of disciplines and good practices. According to MQA (2018a), the specified procedures and guidelines establish standards for higher education, within which a specific HEI can creatively develop its program and effectively allocate resources in alignment with its educational objectives and learning outcomes. The program standards delineate the expected level of achievement for each measure and act as indicators of performance at two levels of attainment: benchmarked standards and enriched standards. The nine areas of evaluation include vision, mission, educational goals and learning outcomes; curriculum design and delivery; learner assessment; learner support services; academic personnel; educational resources; program supervision and appraisal; leadership, governance, and administration; and Continuous Quality Improvement (CQI) (MQA, 2018a).HEIs recognize that each is in different stages of progress, and hence, quality improvement in QA is a continuous process. The performance indicators of quality are thus operationally defined, and the broad aim of higher education is to yield generally educated graduates. To ensure goals are attained in this aspect, HEIs are accountable for planning, designing and implementing programs that are appropriate to the missions and goals. Looking through the lens of implementing LA, to what extent the guidelines on criteria and standards of COPPA and COPIA can be achieved as planned to suit their distinctive purposes? Mokhtar et al. (2012) have conducted a survey on the preparedness among MQA committee toward MQA administration in order to put into effect a CQI in their organizations. The results indicate that 83% of respondents are prepared for Continuous Quality Improvement (CQI). To support this preparedness, five key dimensions have been identified: staff attention and usage of team process; understanding of process; use of information in decision-making; general understanding of quality and needs and wants of customers; and ability of the management to lead. In the context of study, there comes a coherent effort to weigh the stakeholders' interest and other challenges, making LA toward achieving QA of higher education in Malaysia.

In this study, precise benchmarks of the standards will be indicated for the main relevant assessment areas, giving the understanding that fundamentally an HEI must prove that it has fulfilled all benchmark principles for its program but on the other hand to also consider adaptability and acknowledgment of multiplicity to assist the innovative department of education (MQA, 2018a). Throughout the entire transformation process of education shifts of HEIs in Malaysia, test and written exams have been found to be unauthentic to access and evaluate psychomotor and affective learning domain and soft skills; weaknesses are recognized if we solely carry assessment based on test and exams; test are basically unable to measure as a whole the knowledge, attributes which are various and diverse; and quizzes and examinations using paper and pencil, are only useful in testing Cognitive domain of the lower order, that needs memorization and recalling (MQA, 2018b).

Hence, issues on "How do we know how to teach a learning outcome" and "How do we know what types of assessment to use for a learning outcome" are being answered by constructive alignment (CA) of aligning learning outcomes, teaching and learning strategy and assessment strategies (MQA, 2018b). Essentially, with all the data on individual students, personalized learning outcomes can be effectively achieved and measured based on the QA procedures and to achieve PLO meets with CLO or graduates' attributes in that sense. The following sections can further support the understanding of the QA system.

- **Program's Aims and Objectives With Learning Outcomes**

  The standard of programs is eventually evaluated by the capability of the learner to perform their expected accountabilities and roles in social order. Program's aims and objectives reflect wants of the learners (MQA, 2018b). The earlier must be able to meet the later where the objectives, aims and learning outcomes must be informed to students and all stakeholders. Certainly the vital components of the outcome of PEO are developed parallel with the nationwide and worldwide development and must essentially be consistent with, in reassuring of the HEI's vision and mission. In principle, according to MQA (2018b), programs must clarify the competencies that students ought to exhibit on conclusion of the program which include components as stated as MQF namely knowledge and understanding; cognitive skills; functional work skills with focus on practical skills, interpersonal skills, communication skills, digital skills, numeracy skills, leadership, autonomy and responsibility; personal and entrepreneurial skills; and ethics and professionalism (MQA, 2018b). All in all, PEO must be able to be mapped with PLO, PLO to be mapped with MQF learning outcome domain, CLO to be mapped with PLO and assessed based on Bloom's New Taxonomy domains, CLO to be mapped with teaching methods/modes of assessment, and course modules to be mapped with CLO and teaching and learning activities/SLT.

- **Implementation of Curriculum**

  Curriculum means the prearrangement of classes that are planned for a specific period and learning capacity to attain the indicated learning outcomes and commonly leading to an award of a qualification (MQA, 2018a). In it, CA is about bringing learners to take accountability for their personal learning, and forming trust among learners and instructor. With implementation of curriculum, educators should have a clear idea of what students should have a distinct indication of what learners should be able to carry out at the conclusion of a component of learning, and informing this envisioned learning outcomes to learners so that they can at least partake in obligation of attaining them. Program design and delivery method are then to be reviewed and evaluated to meet the benchmark standards, and should be enhanced via needs analysis and other mode of feedback including market, alumni, peers and international experts for the purpose of curriculum improvement, especially to refine learners' experiences and nurture individual growth and obligation as an individual (MQA, 2018b).

- **Assessment Methods**

Relationship between assessment and learning outcome is an important component where assessment principles, approaches and practices are balanced to attainment of the PLO consistent with MQF level. Where assessment is the process that appraises the knowledge, understanding and skills of the students, its principle methods and practices are thus compatible with PEO to promote learning (MQA, 2018b). The criteria of student assessment are thus to be communicated to students at the commencement of the program so that assessment can make available data about knowledge and skills learners have as they move into a class.

Make available dependable information on learner learning and data from learner evaluation and make available data richer on the effects of the program of study/teaching method, provide proof that academic staff make a difference in student learning. In addition, faculty members are able to give a bigger picture of learner needs and achievements (MQA, 2018b). In addition to that suitable knowledge, discerning skills, hands-on skills and skills for life and job can be measured by their capability to clarify, identify, narrate, deliberate the thoughts in the module; capacity to relate, study, compare, query, dispute, differentiate between thoughts and they are related to an evaluation; the capacity to develop, deliberate, redefine, recommend other possibilities, re-conceptualize, incorporate, form new networks; abilities to assess, judge, appraise, criticize the ideas; capability to formulate examinations utilizing applicable resources to highlight the issues; provide proof of rational planning and managing of time in organizing for evaluation; provide proof of team/group in doing the work; capacity to slog in time constrain surroundings; and the usage of suitable skills for problem-solving. Mapping of MQF Learning outcome domain to the assessment of PLO as mentioned earlier is to be monitored and evaluated via mode of assessment such as exams, assignments, project papers, presentations, team projects, group presentations, review of case studies, research, observation study and also specific content reviews (MQA, 2018b).

Moreover, Fischer (2015) wrote that learning is more than being taught where calibration media could make information relevant to the job at hand, in doing so decreasing the problem of data overloading or the necessity for decontextualized learning. Lifelong learning as concluded by Fischer (2015) is to be supported by new technologies in assessment such as visualization, critiquing so that people experience knowledge in new ways. Group discussion, discussion during meals and discussion in classrooms have the possible chances in which knowledge is shaped and created by groups of common students. Fischer (2015) reiterated that we cannot have society to live in a 21st-century world utilizing 19th-century technology.

- **Learning and Teaching Strategies**

  To achieve the desired learning outcome, innovative and active modes of teaching and learning are normally employed. Evaluation and monitoring method are also important aspects of pedagogy and good teaching delivery in evaluation process. In this instance, students will be given Program Module Implementation Plan for self-preparation and planning and to be responsible for their own learning.

Buyarski et al. (2017) in their research raised queries about what way is the best to use analytics to back learners in charge of their individual learning and achievement/success. The LA system had therefore made available a variation of uses of the information, especially in Indiana University in its case. Intervention may be necessary, along with a reorganization based on factors such as student demographics, academic offerings, and university housing capacity. The creation of learning, accomplishment, achievement, and graduation initiatives is intricate.

5.3 Emerging Policies and Directions of Malaysian Higher Education

In recent years, due to rapid economic and social transformations, higher education institutions must be dedicated to preparing learners for jobs that may not yet exist, technologies that may not have been developed, and unforeseen obstacles that may arise (OECD, 2011). Learning and teaching are among the primary contemporary trends in higher education institutions, where quality assurance is evaluated based on the standards aligned with the Academic Quality Assurance (AQA) system (Grapragasem et al., 2014). The AQA framework emphasizes the importance of continuous improvement and stakeholder engagement to ensure that educational offerings meet established quality standards. The purpose of the study is to utilize the hiatus regarding contemporary learning and teaching challenges to adapt to the changes and needs of the Malaysia Education Blueprint, 2015–2025. (MOE, 2015).

Developing nations and those with transitional economies are at risk of further marginalization in a competitive global knowledge economy (The World Bank, 2003). That is because their education system is preparing students with the abilities they require. Legislators must implement necessary reforms to promote new forms of learning that involve generating, applying, analyzing, and synthesizing information, as well as fostering lifelong collaborative learning According to the World Bank Report (The World Bank, 2003), establishing a workforce capable of competing in a global economy; adapting education to meet the lifelong requirements of learners; managing a lifelong learning framework; funding lifelong education; and a future agenda, which can be accomplished through various methods. A quality assurance system is essential for evaluating pupils, and learning outcomes must be tracked efficiently. The World Bank (2003) asserts that a quality assurance system must differentiate between various formal and informal learning contexts and provide opportunities for students to demonstrate their newly acquired skills and knowledge. This differentiation is essential to ensure that the quality assurance framework is inclusive and reflective of diverse educational experiences, so that to ensure that students can effectively demonstrate their competencies in ways that align with both academic standards and real-world applications. The emergence of technological breakthroughs associated with the Fourth Industrial Revolution (4IR) necessitates a comprehensive reevaluation of higher education curricula, emphasizing robotics, artificial intelligence, the Internet of Things, and other relevant fields, particularly on their economic and environmental implications (Penprase, 2018). It provides employees not only with the skills of creating new operations/applications and goods but is also able to integrate the results of this technology on humanity in the ethical use of science and technology. Hence, academic educators have to confront the same changes, and HEIs are bound to undergo the necessary adaptations, although many seem not willing to accept the full content of the facts (Wagner & Wallner, 2016).

Hence, when rethinking academic education to meet these future challenges, a set of propositions to describe fundamental principles to be followed should be developed if we desire to prepare our learners for the future. The ongoing advancement of Academic Quality Assurance (AQA) systems in higher education has led to the development of Individualized Continuous Grade Point Average (ICGPA) and personalized learning approaches, aligning with the learning outcomes expected of 21st-century students. This focus on quality education is a key sustainable development goal outlined in the Ministry of Education's blueprint (MOE, 2015), emphasizing the importance of adapting educational practices to meet contemporary needs and expectations. LA serves as a crucial component in the curricular material and the execution of higher education and in the Ten Shifts of the Malaysia Education Blueprint 2015–2025 (MOE, 2015).

Given that educational quality is paramount for higher education institutions (Sallis, 2002), it is vital to investigate quality assurance and analytics to enhance the student experience. This is where analytics derived from the learners' learning surroundings provide new insights into the students' experience (Boarden & Coates, 2017). Boarden and Coates (2017) assert that their study in Australia on student analytics and student experience indicates that the application of information should extend beyond micro-level communications and educational interventions in learning analytics; instead, student analytics should also focus on enhancing and personalizing the overall learner experience, which is considerably important. Successful student experiences have been attained through innovative methods of understanding higher education and learner experiences, particularly through the identification of a model comprising nine qualities derived from communications and interactions between organizational providers and learners, which contribute to the success of the student experience. Crenshaw (1989), as cited by Boarden and Coates (2017), introduces the concept of intersectionality, which educators should consider as an additional beneficial framework. This construct emphasizes the interconnectedness of various social identities and how they shape individual experiences, particularly in understanding issues of inequality and discrimination. By acknowledging intersectionality, educators can better address the diverse needs of their students and create more inclusive learning environments (Boarden & Coates, 2017). These studies can be further examined within the context of Malaysia, particularly given its multi-ethnic composition. As a whole, the start of learner/student analytics therefore offers a chance for researchers to distance themselves from outdated conceptions. Simultaneously, it helps to reserve the robust framework of LA theories to practice. Acknowledging exactly how probable learners are to success or fail does not deliver actionable data on how to assist learners. Student analytics has emerged as an essential instrument for comprehending the reasons behind subpar student performance, while also enabling educators to implement effective interventions. Cultural stereotypes and the dominance of connections in educational environments are significant factors. Student analytics can foster the development of a more relevant model of learner experience that plays a crucial role in shaping students' future lives, both individually and collectively.

5.4 Conclusion

In conclusion, reviews were conducted based on the impact on teaching and learning, consistent with the framework of the study's conception. LA plays a crucial role in the curriculum content and implementation of higher education, as outlined in the Malaysia Education Blueprint 2015–2025, particularly in addressing the demands and transformations associated with the Fourth Industrial Revolution and its ramifications. The stakeholders acknowledge the critical role of LA in the Malaysia Education Blueprint (2015–2025) but recognize the uncertainty surrounding its long-term impact on pedagogy and student outcomes in the upcoming MHEB (2026–2035).

QA is the means by which an institution guarantees that the standards and values of the scholastic provision are being sustained and improved with confidence and certainty. The QA system of the country in the context of globalization, internationalization and transformation in redressing the environment of learning and teaching is to become accustomed to the shifting surroundings. Through the lens of LA, to what extent guidelines on criteria and standards of COPIA and COPIA can be achieved accordingly to fit their distinct purpose? Statement of program's aims and objectives with learning outcome; implementation of curriculum assessment methods/strategies; and learning and teaching strategies were reviewed.

References

Borden, V. M. H., & Coates, H. (2017). Learning analytics as a counterpart to surveys of student experience. *New Direction for Higher Education, 19*(Fall). Wiley Periodicals, Inc. https://doi.org/10.1002/he.20246.

Brennan, J., & Shah, T. (2000). *Managing quality in higher education: An international perspective on institutional assessment and change*. British Standard Institution.

British Standard Institution. (1991). *Quality vocabulary part 2: Quality concepts and related definitions*. BSI.

Buyarski, C., Murray, J., & Torstrick, R. (2017). Learning analytics across a state wide system. In J. Zilvinskis & V. Boarder (Eds.), *Learning analytics in higher education. New directions for higher education, 179* (Fall). Jossey-Bass.

Chinomona, R. (2013). *Elements of quality assurance at institutions of higher education: Vaal University of technology in South Africa*. https://www.researchgate.net/publication/257928331_Elements_of_Quality_Assurance_at_Institutions_of_Higher_Education_Vaal_University_of_Technology_in_South_Africa

ESIB. (2002). *European student handbook on quality assurance in higher education*. http://www.aic.lv/bolona/Bologna/contrib/ESIB/QAhandbook.pdf

Fischer, G. (2015). Lifelong learning – more than training. Special Issue on "intelligent system/tools in training and life-long learning". *International Journal of Continuing Engineering Education and Life-Long Learning* (Riichiro Mizoguchi & Piet A. M. Kommers, Eds.). http://l3d.cs.colorado.edu/~gerhard/papers/lll99.pdf

Grapragasem, S., Krishnan, A., & Mansor, A. N. (2014). Current trends in Malaysia higher education and the effect on education policy and practice: An overview. *International Journal of Higher Education, 3*, 85. https://doi.org/10.5430/ijhe.v3n1p85

Malaysian Qualifications Agency. (2017). *Malaysian qualifications framework (MQF)* (2nd ed.). http://pps.utem.edu.my/phocadownloadpap/2018%20MQF%202nd%20Edition%2002042018.pdf

Malaysian Qualifications Agency. (2018a). *Code of Practice for Programme Accreditation* (2nd ed.). Retrieved from https://www2.mqa.gov.my/qad/garispanduan/COPPA/2019/Oct/26092019%20CLEAN%20COPPA%202nd%20Edition%20(2017).pdf

Malaysian Qualifications Agency. (2018b). *COPIA form: MQA-03 (Self-Review Portfolio)* (2nd ed.). Retrieved from http://www.mqa.gov.my/portalMQAv3/borang/copia/MQA-03

Ministry of Higher Education. (2015). *Malaysia education blueprint 2015–2025 (higher education)* (Malaysia, Ministry of Higher Education, Putrajaya).

Ministry of Higher Education. https://www.um.edu.my/docs/default-source/about-um_document/media-centre/um-magazine/4-executive-summary-pppm-2015-2025.pdf?sfvrsn=

Mok, K. H. (2011). Impact of globalization: A study of quality assurance system in higher education in Hong Kong and Singapore. *Comparative Education Review*, *44*(20), 148–174.

Mokhtar, R., Jaafar, N. H., Sukiman, S. A., & Rahman, A. B. A. (2012). Continuous quality improvement (CQI) readiness towards Malaysian quality assurance (MQA). In *International conference on management, economics and finance proceeding* (pp. 231–241).

OECD. (2017, April 15). *21st century skills: Learning for the digital age*. https://www.oecd-forum.org/users/50593-oecd/posts/20442-21st-century-skills-learning-for-the-digital-age

Pavel, A. P. (2012). The importance of quality in education in an increasing knowledge-driven society. *The International Journal of Academic Research in Accounting, Finance and Management Sciences*, *2*(1), 120–127, ISSN 2225–8329. www.hrmars.com/journals

Penprase, B. E. (2018). *The Fourth Industrial Revolution and higher education* (pp. 207–229). Higher Education in the Era of the Fourth Industrial Revolution. https://link.springer.com/chapter/10.1007/978-981-13-0194-0_9

Pillay, H. (2002). Understanding learner-centredness: Does it consider the diverse needs of individuals? *Studies in Continuing Education*, *24*(1), 93–102.

Sallis, E. (2002). *Total quality management in education* (3rd ed.). Kogan Page Ltd. http://repository.embuni.ac.ke/bitstream/handle/123456789/1274/[Edward_Sallis]_Total_Quality_Management_in_Educat(BookSee.org).pdf?sequence=1

Susan, R. (2008). Malaysia education: Strategic branding leads to growth in international student number 2006–8. *GlobalHigherEd*. www.globalhighered.wordpress.com

Wagner, G., & Wallner, T. (2016). *Academic education 4.0. conference paper: END 2016 international conference on education and new development, at Ljublijana*. https://www.researchgate.net/publication/ 304115292_ACADEMIC_EDUCATION_40

The World Bank. (2003). *Lifelong learning in the global knowledge economy challenges for developing countries. A World Bank report*. The World Bank Washington, D.C. Retrieved from http://siteresources.worldbank.org/INTLL/Resources/Lifelong-Learning-in-the-Global-Knowledge-Economy/lifelonglearning_GKE.pdf

6 LA and QA – How Does It Matter?

6.1 Introduction

This chapter unveils the "importance of understanding LA to students' learning processes and learning outcomes in achieving QA of higher education in Malaysia", specifically in the context of students' achievement, viability and sustainability of transformation toward achieving QA. The implementation of LA is being considered as a transformative change program in line with the Malaysia Education Blueprint (2015–2025). The impact on institutional diversity has to be matched not only with the QA system of the country but also across national borders to a certain extent to where transformation has to do with redressing the environment of learning and teaching. Therefore, the motivation to explore LA as a continuous evaluation process is crucial, as the journey towards achieving QA involves implementing LA.

6.2 The Tug of War Between LA and QA

Figure 6.1 shows the 3S for LA to QA, which was derived from the concept model of Lim (2021) in Chapter 2. This model was emerged to illustrate the comprehensive critical success factors that enable a more effective implementation of Learning Analytics (LA) for achieving Quality Assurance (QA) in higher education institutions (Lim, 2021). The model consists of three domains:

- The interest of stakeholders is the first tier of the model. Three main ideas were identified, which are benefits to stakeholders, ethical issues and LA as values in students' learning processes and learning outcomes. Core stakeholders focus on benefits that LA can offer to sustain adopting LA effectively and ethically in the long run, with several ingrained values in LA.
- Understanding of issues pertaining to students in their learning processes and outcomes could serve as a guideline to LA intervention. As far as curriculum and learning processes with new learning tools are concerned, HEIs have to work toward solving the bigger and bigger challenges with the involvement of students as well as other change agents. Issues

DOI: 10.4324/9781003584520-6

contributing to viability and sustainability in terms of foreseen resistance to recommended reformation strategies were raised. Thus, one distinctive feature is the term "determinative". This model proposes that a "determinative approach" could be the key to reducing the gaps among LA and QA. Together with this element, several variables were placed to support how implementation can be successful with the adoption of this "determinative approach", impacting LA toward achieving QA in Malaysia.

- The third domain is the output and central focus of this research study: Is LA for QA? For this to be actualized, stakeholders' perspective should be clear along with the adoption of the "determinative approach". Here, one should be very clear about the emerging ideas in the lens of the stakeholders, LA tool for QA, and most significantly the risks to be overcome across the case. In fact, various appraised research studies on benefits and intervention of LA exist, likewise QA, but there appears to be very little evidence on the LA achieving standards of QA. Hence, it is recommended that if the mechanism of "determinative approach" is to be implemented, LA for QA may be feasible at optimum levels.

The extent to which LA contributes to QA in higher education can be summarized by the interrelationships depicted in Figure 6.2, which can be distilled into three components: Students' Academic Experience, Successful Implementation of LA and Strategic Direction (Lim, 2021). LA can successfully achieve QA with the proposed determinative approach including a subset of three focal

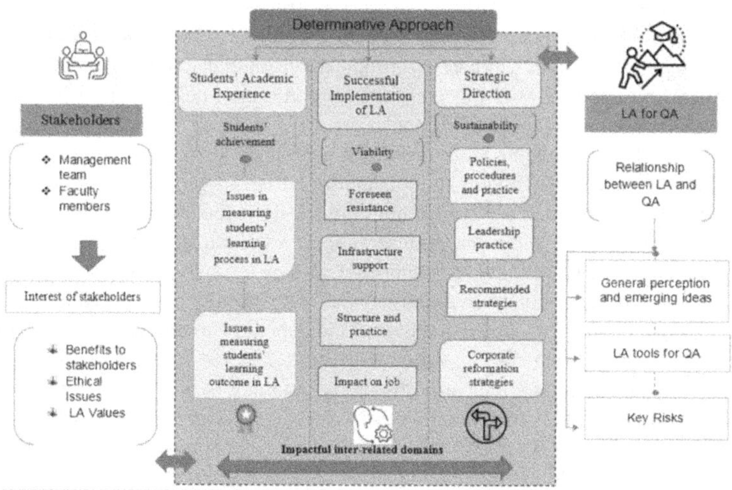

Figure 6.1 3S Learning Analytics Model to Quality Assurance

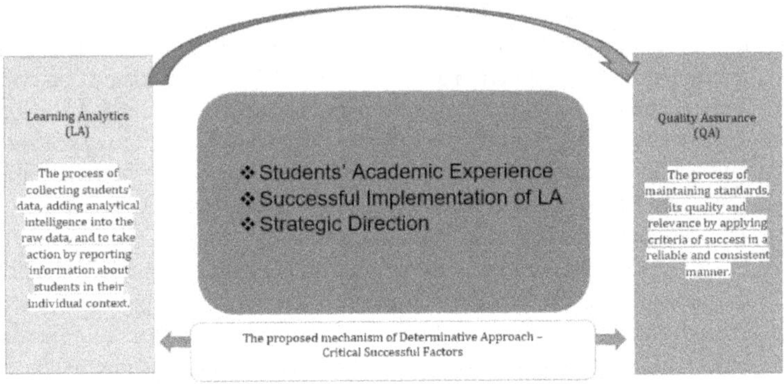

Figure 6.2 Emerged Framework of Inter-Relationship Between LA and QA

elements. All three entities are subsets of the implementation of LA. It signifies the impact of LA on QA in students' educational experiences; although they are distinct, there is some degree of overlap in their interventions. The conclusion is derived from the significant important success aspects. The significance of students' learning experiences, their feasibility and sustainability. They ought to adopt LA to enhance the future sustainability of QA in higher education, particularly for students' academic experiences and achievements. Ultimately, this synthesizes effective teaching and learning on the technological platform such as online learning where teaching pedagogies, adoption of technology, student workload, student assessments and other indicators come into place.

On the whole, LA has yet to redeem its promises fully. On that notion, the deployment of LA projects through a substantial number of strategies (even simultaneously) is indeed crucial, upon which policies are to be laid in more detailed themes. The incorporation of a broad vision of academic excellence, good judgment of investment potential and the full engagement of faculties are crucial. In view that managing HEIs is a very complicated task, institutions would require buy-in not only from the faculty but also from the leadership of staff and management and even the students themselves. All stakeholders must be clear on what problem they are striving to resolve, how glitches can be explained cumulatively and who can aid to unravel the snags.

Educators have to establish that they are dependable caretakers of respectable-value higher education, while functioning that they are reliable providers of good-quality higher education, while functioning in an intricate situation, with various stakeholders, individually with their own anticipations (government, management, faculties, students and parents). To accomplish performance in teaching and learning in accordance with the National Higher Education Strategic Plan (MOE, 2015), the attainment of Excellence in Phase 3 and Beyond 2020 Glory and Sustainability in Phase 4 of the plan may not yet be realized. To be more effectively competing for students against the greater students' achievement, increase of the efficiency of learning processes has become more stringent, especially in funding constraints for private HEIs in Malaysia. Besides technology being an important consideration, human factors, especially the integrated culture in using data and analytics by all LA stakeholders – are essential for successful implementation; therefore, the proposed mechanism of a determinative approach is critical for long-term success.

6.3 Discussion on the Determinative Approach

6.3.1 LA and QA – How Do They Matter to Students?

6.3.1.1 Students' Learning Processes

It is challenging to understand how theory and analytics relate to move "from clicks to constructs" in a principled way (Knight & Buckingham Shum, 2013). Also, according to Knight and Buckingham Shum (2013), "LA are a specific incarnation of the bigger shift to an algorithmically pervaded society, and their wider impact on education needs careful consideration" (p. 17). As put forward by Knight, Buckingham Shum and Littleton in 2014, the theoretical and practical purposes of such heuristics are twofold: first, they support assessment and pedagogy grounded in epistemology (organized hierarchically); second, they are represented in a Venn diagram format, where increased overlap signifies greater complementarity of the theorized position (Knight et al., 2014). An example given in the review was that LA has the potential to marginalize students who are weak in critical-thinking skills, so alternative ways of engaging activities should be introduced. Based on the findings of the research study, this fundamentally is perceived as a deployment for tools to express a commitment to a particular educational worldview designed to nurture a particular kind of learner, such as personalized learning.

Alongside that, the theory of "knowledge" is retrieved and reviewed in relation to issues of learning and teaching, reflecting the local context. In addition, past review, from p. 16 and p. 47 of Theobald's study, conducted in 2009 (as cited in Williams, 2017), shows that John Dewey is one of the most influential educational philosophers known to date. Despite the current educational emphasis in the United States on implementing Common Core standards and administering standardized tests and state examinations, which may present challenges according to John Dewey's theories, Williams (2017) highlighted Dewey's concept of social learning, emphasizing that students are distinct learners who thrive in authentic social environments. Consequently, challenges in assessing students' learning processes are rooted in learning theory. A gap is seen based on research findings on the different education system between high school and HEIs. Where William (2017) in his study has concluded that the main focus of John Dewey's classroom learning is that more than preparing students for passing standardized exams and state assessments, especially with more and more 21st-century classrooms. In the United States, even though so, classrooms are still placing an emphasis on the importance and relevance to community-building relationship and developing higher-level thinking skills for real-life application. Student-centered learning is where educators can see much of John Dewey's social learning theory viewing classroom as a social entity to learn and to solve problems as a community.

As students' classrooms gets bigger each day, students' learning processes need to be understood better, including their progression in learning. That is where new phenomenon emerged that LA is to improvise student learning experience so as to meet end needs on time. QA exists side by side to support the principle of "fitness for the purpose" in education, ensuring that it effectively prepares students to become responsible citizens and lifelong learners. To guarantee that students acquire and can apply knowledge relevant to their future careers, HEIs must ensure that students achieve learning outcomes, provided that HEIs adhere to and comply with established QA and standards.

For a student on the other hand, does this matter? We understand that there is always a learning gap between high school and tertiary education in Malaysia in terms of knowledge base as well as learning style, put aside the emotional stability due to change of environment. Berry (2017) found out that academic level, academic load and the terms of enrollment are also predictive measures. Coherently from the research findings from interviews supported by document analysis, enrolling students with the right entry requirement helps in the LA process in terms of having LA to benchmark QA.

Learning will always be made easier by facilitators if the information on who you are and where you are from is made available. If guidance can be rendered easily, then the learning process will be made more conducive. Where students' learning pace and path can be adjusted so that one can learn faster in the right context of strength, as well as to accommodate the weaker at a normal pace, personalized learning in short is helpful. So many other issues, such as generic knowledge gained, may not be actual in the sense that skills learned may not be applicable in the workplace, especially where constructivist and connectivism approaches to education where students build on what they know by asking questions, investigating, interacting with others and reflecting on these experiences, thereby acknowledging real-life learning as messy and complex. As such, effective learning prepares students for learning for the rest of their lives.

6.3.1.2 Students' Learning Outcomes

Previous discussion prompted researchers to look into learning theories where LA facilitates constructivism and connectivism learning. Besides, what about non-cognitive skills, such as leadership skills and ethical sense that the MOE is particularly concerned with, and how will students be evaluated based on the new five clusters of the MQF domain (MQA, 2018)? The case study examines the feasibility and methods of measuring this through LA as individuals acquire knowledge. Monitoring students' performance in real time during their growth is an exemplary feedback mechanism, enabling students to maximize limited resources to achieve maximum results. Ultimately, Ultimately, human intervention in LA will assist lecturers in comprehending students more effectively, particularly regarding stress management, teamwork abilities, and critical thinking. Indeed, this finding is supported by Scalter and Mullan (2017): that is, isolation of influence of LA may not be useful in measuring effectiveness when it is part of broader benefits to mend data-based procedures in an organization as a whole.

Relatively, "grades" or "marks" of assessment mean everything if we are talking about meeting learning outcome per se. Moreover, living in a knowledge society where time is fluid, knowledge does not last. As put forward by Granados (2015), Elmes (2017) and Bates (2015), effective learning to enhance knowledge transfer and knowledge management is important. Viewing it from a different perspective, "marks" or "grade" may merely be a benchmark. Whether or not students meet the end needs in acquiring future skills, it is beyond QA or LA, as they are not meant for the future world.

Learning prepares students to handle situations in an indefinite future based on present-day understanding. As cited by Srikanthan and Dalrymple (2002), in Ewell (1997), an "ideal system" should incorporate the learning insights in academic programs and systems; these insights include transforming students, learner as an epistemologist, learning opportunity, learning well from the perspective of difficulty, responses/feedback and learning in an interpersonal context. In that sense, findings were further supported by participants on transfer of knowledge and acquisition of different levels of knowledge with LA. For instance, generic attainment of outcome may not be the actual attainment. Namoun et al. (2021) in their research reviewed 62 relevant papers for the period 2010–2020 to predict students' learning outcomes, such as grades (by adopting smart techniques). The studies focused on the models used, how learning outcomes are predicted and the factors influencing them. The findings revealed that few areas such as student grades, students' online activities and students' academic emotions were reflected to be the most predictive for learning outcomes. Indeed, further research was called to address issues in this area.

LA is a tool for educators and learners; researchers are still working hard to obtain a "robust" measure of learning in the application of "big data" approaches. After all, in many aspects, LA certainly improves the process of QA, leading the education system in Malaysia to greater heights. Although applications of LA are at infancy in Malaysia, its presence is being felt, and it is not ignored by students. Ultimately, there is a saying, "The success of students is the success of HEI". Given the growing importance of LA in students' learning processes and learning outcomes, Malaysian HEIs need to understand that it is vital for them to know LA's contributions.

6.3.2 Benefits and Interest of Stakeholders

6.3.2.1 Benefits

This study proposes two approaches of stakeholder theory. One is of Burrow's multiple lenses approach (1999), distinguishing stakeholders in HEIs based on location and involvement status, potential for cooperation and threats, and individual stakeholder's stake and influences on the institutions. The other is Mitchell et al.'s (1997) theory on stakeholder credential and reputation, which consist of ideas of power, lawfulness and insistence. In the local context, stakeholders of private HEIs in Malaysia are primarily the government, which is represented by the ministry, the management, the faculties, students and parents, who consistently face challenges arising from managing best practice for the maximum benefits of students in the best environment.

Having to explore the extent to which LA tools to achieve QA particularly in measuring students' learning processes and students' learning outcomes, the stakeholders of the understudied is framed to Management and the member of Faculties (Lim, 2021).

Pistilli (2017) supports stakeholders' interest in the benefits derived from the LA intervention for data monitoring for feedback systems. In reviewing the literature of this study, it is essential to reference social cognitive theory, which posits that feedback is a crucial mechanism for informing students about the actions necessary to attain CLO (Bandura, 1997). Students are motivated by a specific desired outcome, which instructors can facilitate through a LA-driven intervention. Unfortunately, the research findings did not indicate if lengthy feedback is generally unsuccessful; instead, as Clow (2012) notes, the evaluation of immediate efforts like intervention is critical rather than accessing the outcome of LA. Empirical evidence indicates a decrease in attrition rates, and research findings demonstrate that enhancements in student outcomes therefore lower attrition rates. Furthermore, it aids in formulating criteria for policy development regarding the use of Lain addition to the review of literature in the earlier chapter, Shimada et al. (2018) have conducted a study on simultaneous/real-time LA systems for enhancement of on-site lessons. Extensive research using a simultaneous/real-time analytics grid was conducted, and outcomes showed that students could adjust the pace of their lecturer based on the real-time response system. This also resulted in encouraging students to emphasize and save key words and phrases. Teachers should consider this new strategy to enhance their instruction effectively. The researchers focused on LA as a resource to assist teachers and learners in enhancing their educational practices. And one vital concern in LA is attaining response for enhancing the learning surroundings and learners themselves. The real-time feedback is provided on a weekly or monthly basis as analysis, rather than providing immediate feedback to on-site teachers/students, since LA is fundamentally conducted after school terms or class sessions. So, Shimada et al. (2018) focused on feedback from on-site classrooms, even during lectures that had not been previously considered, which pertained to the on-site educational environment. They employed both an e-learning approach and an e-book method to facilitate concurrent learning activities during the lectures, which were adjusted to the existing conditions in the physical classroom. Based on this literature, it was also found out from the research findings that real-time feedback is essential, as rectification would be too late. However, to what extent this is an important aspect to encourage drive and contentment of both teachers and students are to be further researched, also evaluations in the cognitive and pedagogic fields as highlighted in previous research.

6.3.2.2 Ethics

Malaysian academics seem to express higher level of doubts on the ethics of data, such as what data to collect and for what purpose (West et al., 2018). It is the amount of personal data, the extent of processing of the storage, accessibility and information flow that need to be monitored so that privacy rights are protected (Hoel & Chen, 2016; Nissenbaum, 2010). Those problems were clearly articulated based on the findings of the research investigation. Furthermore, the results indicated that a comprehensive list of requirements for LA systems must be formulated according to appropriate guidelines. It was determined that it is crucial to restrict access to information for individuals lacking legitimate entitlement to it. As supported by Nissenbaum (2010), information on attendance, discipline and disability could be seen as intrusive to a certain extent, necessitating consent as an essential feature to avoid privacy violations, especially during the university flow of information from one campus to another.

An ethical concern identified in the research findings remains unexamined by the researcher. Future research may be undertaken on that specific concept. Human intervention, a significant factor, has emerged concerning the appropriate capture of information on students' learning, a topic inadequately addressed in the literature study. The findings revealed a contrasting perspective to Johnson (2017), indicating that LA is perceived as a tool for predicting information for individual students, although no decisions were made regarding the specific student. Johnson (2017) empirically asserted that recognizing students' uniqueness in LA is problematic, as LA often fails to engage with individuals and instead produces data collections that merely attempt to categorize them. In other words, dehumanization is imposed on students as official resolutions are formulated not based on the humanistic complexities of social and individual contexts, but through mechanistic systems of measurement, classification, and response.

6.3.2.3 Values

According to Dix and Leavesley (2015), the essential crucial elements involved in LA are clearly data, analysis and actions. Where analytical intelligence is added to the raw data through algorithms, ultimate action would be the goal of LA process. Interestingly, several values identified in the findings from the stakeholders' perspective were insufficiently addressed by prior studies. For example, as discussed by a participant, the merits of LA can be more accurately assessed through pedagogical approaches that facilitate the collection of structured data via problem-based learning. Furthermore, LA offers precise, immediate and essential information regarding the individual, incorporating motivational aspects into the analysis. The findings indicated that data obtained from recorded qualitative human interactions enhance the projected level of expertise. This is also evident in the discovery of an individual participant's personal experience of LA to ascertain the most effective methods for student learning in online classes, which aided her in comprehending students' needs as a facilitator.

6.3.3 Viability – Are We There Yet?

6.3.3.1 Foreseen Resistance to Change

The viability of LA being put into practice toward achieving QA is the main topic of discussion here. The findings showed that resistance to change and adaptability of the stakeholders toward LA also plays an acute part in establishing positive contributions to QA in HEIs. As supported by Rick (2013), The issue revolves around the collective conviction regarding the necessity for change, the extent to which change complicates the fulfillment of stakeholders' needs, the perception that risks surpass benefits, doubts about the capacity for success, skepticism regarding the efficacy of change, concerns about management's handling of change, inconsistencies with core values and, ultimately, the faith in those accountable for implementing change. The results indicate that lecturers' reluctance may stem from their opposition to technology adoption, a factor not adequately addressed in prior research reviews. Nevertheless, some views from the findings were supported by Zhou and Lin (2016) as they wrote that flexibility and adaptability, which are considered to be basis of mental wealth. That was indeed further supported by Ployhart and Bliese in 2006: that is, in order to adjust and adopt to shifting situations, each person has to display adaptableness in both cognition and behavior.

The researcher's in-depth analysis has led to the emergence of a subtheme: resistance to change, particularly in relation to perceptions of individuals within the specific setting of the case university. It is up to how one way of dissecting the relationship between older and young lecturers, passionate or transactional lecturers toward technology savvy and otherwise. In other words, perceptions of individuals are merely reflections of our viewpoints, which do not necessarily align with others' dichotomies.

6.3.3.2 Infrastructural Support

Numerous empirical evidence was discovered that suggests that barriers to successful implementation include a variety of constraints in institutional capacity that are associated with the collection, storage and sharing of data; infrastructure overheads in terms of human resources, software and hardware; the adaptability of dashboards and other data feedback reports for students and instructors; and potential preconceived notions regarding the inference of outcomes. In fact, LA's efforts to achieve success in QA are not limited to the institutional level; they also extend to the learning process. The LA system has to integrate with other data systems at the institutional level and enhance the capacity of teaching practices and students learning support to address infrastructure challenges.

In order to use LA successfully across institutions, pertinent stakeholders ought to be participating from the start in the designing of system, asserted Buyarski et al. (2017). Moreover, vital to the execution of LA are concerns regarding organizational-wide administrative capacity pertaining to obtaining LA tools to all relevant people, ensuring that services and supports are accessible to students with risk issues (Lonn et al., 2012). Although most of the participants shared the same thoughts that infrastructural support is key for effective implementation, some have different views. Interestingly, the understanding of the framework and preparation of timeline to make things come true are, in fact, the pertinent factors identified in the research. Others that are mentioned include a newly integrated system with accompanying training, as well as the availability of required tools and platforms.

6.3.3.3 Structure and Practice to Change

Campbell et al. (2007, p. 42) reported, "Analytics marries large datasets, statistical techniques, and predictive modeling". LA uses both conventional information (taken from surveys, student enrollment records, other traditional data source) and ten new sorts of information stemming from transactional systems such as online courses, LMSs and other networks.

Hence, for the purpose of this research perspective, LA is characterized by Zilvinskis et al. (2017, p. 10) as the process of utilizing real-time information to predict student success, promote engagement through interventions or support based on those predictions, and monitor the impact of those actions. From the research finding, the researcher found out that generically, the overall views shared by participants are realistic. Although the data at this point of time is still fragmented, there is general awareness of the entire landscape of direction of higher education in Malaysia. The interests of shareholder are brought up again here on the impact regarding the effects of government initiatives, management, academics and students on their readiness to adopt LA. That includes adapting to roles in predicting and prescribing of data, keeping up with technology, addressing difficulties as there is no common indicator among departments, assessing stakeholders readiness for change, and acknowledging the fragmentation of current data.

Researchers' in-depth analysis revealed that academics' involvement in LA activity to improve student learning experience is a significant factor, which includes students as well. Although it was not well emphasized in previous literature reviews, conducive digitalization of data collection would alleviate the tedious tasks faced by academics, encompassing their responsibilities as lecturers as well as their involvement in seminars and tutorials, which remain significant factors. Furthermore, to build students' confidence in this tool is essential. Researchers also compared this case with a study examining the experiences of academics in Australia and Malaysia (West et al., 2018), revealing that participants under study of this case university showed interest. No response was received on their perception that the interests of LA is more for higher institutional concerns rather than other attributes to the faculties. One reason may be that the university is currently an analytics-driven entrepreneurial institution, where the mindset of employees is inclined to the reality of change.

Participants' reflections from the research findings indicate that the platform utilized for the integration of instructional tools and systems would be online learning. To attain QA, prior research indicates that LA utilizing the OLI provides a framework for leveraging educational technology to enhance the relationship between pedagogical practices and learning research in improving student outcomes. Thille and Zimmaro (2017) stated that the information obtained from student interactions in flexible learning environments is analyzed and utilized for making pedagogical decisions. Consequently, the system can either autonomously select a learning task for students or provide guidance to the instructor to assess students' competence in achieving specific CLO and the correlation of CLO with PLO, while also aligning with the graduate attributes that comply with the QA standards of the MQA. Primarily, HEIs with numerous campuses that implement immediate alert systems to enhance student success report moderate to high satisfaction among students. (Simmons, 2011). The successful adoption of accepting LA data as a primary guide for intervention necessitates the integration of LA at all levels of HEIs, from senior leadership to faculty members, advisors, and staff who will engage with students using this data (Wagner & Longanecker, 2016). The topic of leadership will be addressed in a subsequent section. Nonetheless, a primary concern of stakeholders is the teaching staff's competence to fulfill the demands of this transition. Furthermore, the integration of instructional elements within a cohesive system necessitates the rethinking of assessment activities for alignment.

6.3.3.4 Impact on Job

One of the critical reasons for staff resistance to change is due to the impact it will have on their job activities during the transformation process. As put forward by Scalter (2017) and Rick (2013), willingness to accept changes relating to job content play a critical role in creating a positive relationship among stakeholders in the integration of LA into the classroom culture, necessitating that management remains mindful of the unwanted effects. The implementation of LA from the perspective of management and faculties showed that no one likes to be given more tasks, which is a common workplace problem today. This is particularly evident in the academic environment, where the additional workload for staff is notable, despite the positive outcomes associated with students acquiring new abilities, which enhance their progress and overall work efficiency. Previous studies provide limited information regarding the implications of LA deployment on the nature of jobs, suggesting that such jobs may become more laborious and constrained in relation to measuring and predicting non-cognitive outcomes. Furthermore, regarding the primary role of academics, it pertains to the idea that educators should prioritize teaching above administrative duties, unless digitalization intervenes. The limited discussion in this section may be attributed to the lack of practical implementation of tools at the example university, resulting in a superficial understanding of the subject. However, implications on the impact in general as well as recommended strategies will be discussed later on in the next sections.

6.3.4 Sustainability – Strategic Direction

Whether or not this transformation will be sustainable depends on this shift associated with corporate strategy and hence new policies, practices and procedures to be formulated and to be executed under right leadership practices and recommended strategies.

6.3.4.1 Policies, Procedures and Practices

Empirical studies showed that LA is implemented using highly diverse approaches in recent years (Gasevic et al., 2016). Predictors and indicators for academic achievement, student engagements and self-controlled learning skills are to be developed. Visualization exploration and interpretation of data prompting remedial action and inception of intervention to outline learning surroundings are facing great challenges to HEIs. This research finding examined how policies and procedures respond to the common voice. However, there are minimum thoughts shared with regard to existing policy management on LA. That may be due to case university currently lacking policies. However, participants thought that policies and processes might be established to integrate transformation efforts into the workload of each academic. Consequently, there will be no concerns regarding micromanagement, execution of staff accountability, or the potential addition of responsibilities to the already burdensome requirements identified in the research findings.. This was indeed further supported by similar problems raised by Scalter (2017), indicating that numerous institutions are confused about the real implementation, notably with the designation of lecturers or tutors as the responsible parties for execution.

6.3.4.2 Leadership Practice

Distributed leadership (DL) is examined here since it is a prominent idea within the research findings of this study based on the analysis of collected works. Empirical studies suggest that the practice of DL is relevant in the rapidly evolving environment of HEIs during significant transitional changes. What is DL? The concept of DL emerged in the late 1990s and early 2000s (Bolden, 2011; Tam, 2018). The findings indicate that leadership practice should be decentralized within specific domains, particularly with HODs possessing substantial knowledge in LA. This aligns with the concept of DL, which posits that no single head of school or leader can effectively manage the complexities of an educational institution, as leaders often focus on what individuals do rather than the underlying reasons and methods behind their actions. (Spillane, 2005). The combined accomplishment of DL strives to fulfill the institution's objectives and the educational goals of the syllabus and curriculum (Spillane et al., 2004). Numerous research studies have increasingly examined DL in relation to the practices, responsibilities and roles of positional leaders, particularly within the educational sector. This concept shares a common theoretical foundation with other leadership models, including democratic leadership, team leadership and shared leadership (Spillane, 2005; Bolden, 2011; Tam, 2018). Teamwork and collaborative teamwork were also found from the research findings.

Spillane and Diamond (2007) wrote that DL is a form of practice rather than a role or responsibility. Spillane (2005) in his practice-centered model delineates leadership practice as a product of the interactions of institutional leaders, followers, and their context. Leadership is defined as the interactions of individuals and their contexts, where these collective interactions co-create numerous leaders. The essence is not in the activities of a leader, but in the interactions among them, which may encompass administrators and specialists. (Spillane, 2005). Spillane (2005) further argued that it is not merely the position that is significant to leadership practice; however, situation also defined leadership practice with respect to heads and their followers. Another attribute of DL is its recognition of interdependence as a key characteristic of communication among leaders. Thompson in 1976 identified three types of interdependency—reciprocal, pooled, and sequential—which serve as the foundation for this concept (Spillane, 2005). All attributes of

DL among management, HODs, subject lecturers, and administrative personnel appear to align with the perspectives of stakeholders as indicated by the research findings. Although findings with regard to the leadership relationship distributed but not power, it is imperative to take heed on the reflection from the perspective of research case with the research done by Harris and Spillane (2008, p. 33) that proposed "it is a way of getting under the skin of leadership practice, of seeing leadership practice differently and illuminating the possibilities for organizational transformation". Bolden (2011) examined the dynamics of power and inspiration, highlighting that inadequate thought may result in the distribution of leadership while power frequently remains centralized. The concept of DL may be proposed by the HOD to enhance commitment and participation in transformation initiatives, potentially creating significant disparities in resource access and power dynamics, which could lead to complications. Although Bolden (2010) suggested that power is intrinsically connected to leadership discourse and practices, it is essential not to overlook the influence of organizational boundaries and context. The practices of the HOD of one department may impact those within another, and the interconnection of flow of students' data may/may not ripple across to impact upon prediction. So, the findings of Spillane (2005) and Bolden (2011) indicate that DL is a perspective for school headship thoughts, not a scheme for compelling leadership for how a school leadership should be carried out in this context. So far there is very little evidence on the effectiveness of DL in implementing LA for QA, which can be crucial (Spillane, 2005; Bolden, 2011). However, it is not whether headship is distributed that is important but, above all, how it is distributed in the research case. Descriptive development is hence vital in establishing the underlying relations between DL, LA and QA in terms of students' learning processes and outcomes.

Looking at Distributed Leadership (DL) through the lens of rhetoric versus reality in the context of significant transitions in higher education—such as the rapid emergence of demands, opportunities, competition, and internationalization—findings from Gosling and Bolden (2009) identify two principal approaches to DL: "devolved," which is associated with top-down inspiration, and "emergent," linked to bottom-up and horizontal inspiration. The study revealed that "devolved" leadership was characterized by interviewees describing formal mechanisms for strategic decision-making and accountability throughout the institution, depicting DL as a practice orchestrated from the top and disseminated across the organization. In contrast, emerging bottom-up practices of shared and informal leadership demonstrated a greater willingness to accept responsibility and generate innovative ideas, recognizing that every individual contributes to the organization's leadership, regardless of formal acknowledgment. This latter approach closely resembles the concept of deep learning as referenced in existing literature (e.g., Spillane, 2005; Harris & Spillane, 2007; Spillane & Diamond, 2007; Bolden, 2009).

However, this emergent approach is less prevalent in data collected from research contexts compared to the findings presented by Gosling and Bolden (2009). Supporting this perspective, Wan (2014) identified DL as encompassing both "top-down" and "bottom-up" initiatives that involve various formal and informal means of communication from the university level down to faculty and department levels. Overall, the study underscores the necessity of striking a balance between these two processes. Ultimately, DL is a political concept; understandings are shaped by how individuals perceive their roles and power within the organization. This complexity often makes it more controversial than initially perceived by senior management.

What remains clear is that DL cannot be replaced by a singular leadership model in higher education, as it does not eliminate the need for official leaders or structural arrangements. Authority and influence arise from individuals and groups in formal roles as well as through informal connections and broader contexts. Visible, personal, and strong leadership is valued when it provides direction and transparency but only when it promotes the mutual well-being of all organizational members. Whether this balance can be achieved remains contested and is a matter of perspective (Gosling & Bolden, 2009). In questioning what DL accomplishes in higher education, Gosling and Bolden highlight that rhetoric plays a crucial role in distinguishing between experiences of leadership and their intended logic. This understanding helps mediate conflicts regarding identity among academics and administrators while providing a broader perspective on the fluctuating values within universities influenced by those who control budgets and academic leadership.

Diamond and Spillane (2016) employed a retrospective framework to explore concepts from a DL perspective, focusing on the evolution of study processes, examination of educational frameworks, and implications of positional disparities in leadership practice. Reflecting on their findings from case studies, the extent to which DL facilitates successful implementation of Learning Analytics (LA) toward Quality Assurance (QA) involves variables related to situational factors aligned with ministry initiatives as well as adaptability to changes in institutional culture, including accommodating diverse stakeholder interests.

DL aims to accomplish the mutual objectives of the organization, and the importance of the leader is to practice rather than to carry out the role or responsibility (Spillane, 2005; Bolden, 2011; Tam, 2018), which means leaders practice interactions between people and their situation where collective interactions are co-enacted by multiple leaders, including faculties and administrators. In this research case, the basis is reciprocal, pooled and sequential. The lecturers have more interactions within the faculty and departments instead of with the senior management. Simultaneously, it disclosed that the authority's influence and engagement in the university's critical trajectory may be diminished at the faculty level, a communication gap between the two stakeholder groups is evident and the dissemination of transformation objectives to the faculties may be inadequate. There is common theoretical basis of this particular concept from others, such as democratic leadership, team leadership and shared leadership (Spillane, 2005; Bolden, 2011; Tam, 2018). DL suggests that authority or power is constantly associated with the practices and discourse of leadership within the context and time.

DL is a practice of "top-down" and "bottom-up" attempts, involving diverse official and casual methods of communications from university level to faculty and department levels. It is a perspective for rationalizing about school leadership, not a proposal for competent leadership. It is not whether leadership is distributed but rather how it is distributed. Definitive building is hence crucial before causative relations between DL, LA and QA in terms of students' learning processes and outcomes can be entrenched. One significant aspect of DL is the identification of principal approaches: "devolved", which is linked to a top-down influence, and "emergent", which is associated with a bottom-up and horizontal effect. DL should be depicted as a practice governed from the top and actively implemented throughout the institution. It is important to note that bottom-up and emergent processes of communal and casual leadership were more inclined to embrace accountability and generate innovative ideas.

6.3.4.3 Recommended Strategies and Corporate Reformation Strategies

Based on all the research findings of the research case study, the recommended strategies and corporate reformation strategies are summarized as follows:

- Policies are to be made and to be compelled to in the first place.
- Flexible government regulations are to be in place.
- Effective leadership practice, self-management of staff and networking horizontally throughout the university, whether by peer pressure or hierarchical pressure due to power, are suggested to be practiced. For instance, a participant mentioned "no shareholders tell me what to learn, did shareholder tell me to learn this and that?"
- It is a continuous journey, and the stakeholders have to start from some point or other.
- Adequate capacity building and preparation and the integration into one system are important critical success factors.
- A strategy for comprehensive guidance aimed at achieving QA should be established for the forthcoming years taking into consideration the way we go forward. Some participants even suggested implementing, beginning from a department in the first year of tertiary programs, while some others suggested to make it compulsory with unsure boundaries.
- It seems that it is desirable to create an extension of a division as the central body to drive LA. It will be generically led by the top management.

- Enforcement of policies will no doubt be a strategic move. That includes policy borrowing and also the adoption for constructive alignment of curriculum with teaching pedagogy and assessment. In fact, the researchers also found the same view from experts' advice in the same context.
- Leading this transition is no longer only a function and obligation; it has become a discipline. The primary responsibility of mid-management is to formulate strategies dictated by the executive level that maximize efficiency. Furthermore, this encompasses the daily responsibilities – the routinization of both academic and administrative tasks.
- LMS is the key platform for LA. To install LA into LMS may be a strategic move.
- Management has to make major decision to buy or not to buy into it. That is because it is the money and the people that will fall in place, which is fundamental.
- Making decisions is beyond faculty; however, faculty members are the one on the ground to make it happen.
- All stakeholders must implement efforts that are culturally aligned with the corporate strategy.

6.3.5 Relationship of LA and QA

The researcher's comprehensive analysis revealed the emergence of the theme about the relationship between LA and QA, with the primary purpose of this study being to assess the effectiveness of LA as a tool in achieving QA in higher education. In this context, research findings indicate that crucial components encompass comprehending the concerns from students' experiences, addressing the hurdles to facilitate viable transformation and ensuring that the change is sustainable in light of key risks and emerging trends.

6.3.5.1 General Perceptions and Emerging Ideas

Researchers agree that public administrations worldwide are seeking higher education to become more responsive to economic and social demands, enhance accessibility at reduced prices, and ensure comparability among institutions. In other words, quality has been utilized as a tool to safeguard compliance in this case.

LA is about using data to monitor students' learning. There is a lack of comprehensive data on the learning process, which could provide more accurate estimations of learning, such as the frequency of logins, time spent on a page, and clickstream data. Likewise, when academics discuss the assessment tasks we design, they must provide reliable evidence to serve as effective processes for the talents that instructors aim to exemplify while also being sufficiently relevant to the theoretical domain of QA. Computer scientists and learning researchers are currently assessing the value of deep learning, which connects synthetic neurons over time, in understanding human knowledge development. They believe that the data sets generated by thousands of students across various contexts, when combined with machine learning algorithms, present a unique opportunity to discover new frameworks for student success. (Thille & Zimmaro, 2017). So, as technology-facilitated learning environments continue to go forward, for sure, academics' capacity to plan and design assessment tasks that are more precise to capture student learning will also progress. The researcher conducted an in-depth examination and determined the significance of understanding specific learning objectives rather than generic ones. When discussing analytics, scholars focus on data and statistics. The research findings indicate that the issue arises when participants are uncertain whether "marks" provide a fair evaluation of learning. What type of data is collected from those marks? These are significant emergent concepts that warrant more investigation. Moreover, data indicated that an ethical concern emerged when the initial input of the guidelines was inaccurate. In actuality, given the circumstances of the case under examination, upgrading the curriculum may not be a straightforward or timely endeavor; hence, maintaining current materials may prove difficult.

LA incorporates the OLI to provide a model using educational technology to change the correlation of research, learning, research and technology drills to improve learning outcomes, including generating meaning of data of learning process to predict success (Thille and Zimmaro, 2017); LA efforts primarily restructure the manner in which HEIs consider student accomplishment through students' learning outcomes and retention in meeting the complete goal (Buyarski et al., 2017); LA's prediction model looks at pre-entry attributes to evaluate risks, helping needy students to reduce risks for course failure and incompletion of program, which in turn reduce burden the cost of education (Pistilli & Arnold, 2010); learners benefit from personalized information in the LA cycle (Clow, 2012); in regard to stakeholders, benefits of LA include reduction of students' attrition rate by monitoring students' learning processes where identification of risk can be detected early, leading to higher achievement rate and lower dropout rate; achievement of cost-effectiveness to the management where LA can be integrated with the LMS for instance; resource (optimization and enhancement of effective communication through real-time feedback; better evaluation on pedagogies and instructional design for quality improvement and assurance (Wong, 2017), the findings indicate that achieving goals in the context of higher education in Malaysia can be realized by prioritizing the enhancement of platforms and tools, as well as optimizing operational processes for LA.

Based on research findings, high school students in Malaysia progress into HEIs through a progression pathway, and a learning gap between high school students and university students has been recorded by previous concepts. That is due to many reasons such as knowledge base, learning styles, teaching pedagogies and others. Hence, barriers on effective predictive and prescriptive measures with LA arise. No data exists regarding prospective students, as lecturers lack insight into their strengths and weaknesses beyond minimum grade information. This project presents a more significant challenge for analytics in the initial year of tertiary education due to little data for evaluation.

The Malaysian Qualifications Agency (MQA) is responsible for the domestic recognition of higher education programs and qualifications, as well as for supervising and regulating quality standards in educational providers. The five clusters of the Malaysian Qualifications Framework (MQF) serve as the principal benchmark, clarifying the academic levels of learning outcomes. The five clusters are namely knowledge and understanding; cognitive skills; functional work skills which focus on practical skills, interpersonal skills, communication skills, digital skills, numeracy skills, leadership, autonomy and responsibility; personal and entrepreneurial skills; and ethics and professionalism (MQA, 2018a). The challenge to the findings was about LA's ability to assess non-cognitive outcomes in learning, in contrast to scientific measures. Furthermore, a primary aspect of LA, which constitutes the central research issue of this study, is the obligation of educationists to furnish graduates with the requisite knowledge and abilities that meet the future demands of the industry. The challenge lies in our potential ignorance regarding future skill requirements.

6.3.5.2 LA as Tools for QA

Researchers have consistently highlighted the advantages of LA for stakeholders, drawing from prior studies and the findings of this case study. Despite LA being a novel innovation in HEIs, numerous concerns persist, particularly regarding non-traditional face-to-face education formats such as online learning. It is intriguing to investigate the extent to which QA is attained through the deployment of LA in a HEIs. QA from the perspective of higher education indicates that the case understudied has so far exceeded, if not maintained, required standards set by the MQA and ISO9001-2015.

Subsequently, the investigation focused on the existence of defined indicators or parameters for diagnosis, prediction, and prescription. As put forward by Thille and Zimmaro (2017), indicated that limited empirical data exists about how LA enhances QA. In this context, the findings contribute to research by suggesting that LA guidelines should be incorporated into QA standards, as the outcomes of QA are evaluated through a QA framework.. LA can assess the achievement of structured learning outcomes. Consequently, QA parameters can be formulated based on the LA framework to diagnose, forecast, and prescribe solutions to address deficiencies in student outcomes. Outcomes are indeed associated with the intervention domains. Generally, LA can provide educators insights into the acquisition of knowledge and values, including students' cognitive skills and their development. However, based on the research findings, perhaps the gap of the inter-relationship between LA and QA can be bridged by many critical factors, such as issues in measuring students' learning outcomes in LA and factors contributing to the success of implementing LA, such as effective leadership practice. In essence, the findings reveal that LA indeed should improve the process of QA, provided the system is properly designed and implemented.

For the sake of discussion, curriculum comprises name, credit values, synopsis, teaching methods, assessment methods, modules and reference books. Stimulatingly, a participant shared the thought that overseas has better LA-built study material, which comes with structured guidelines; as a result, LA in that case is more structured, and that was indeed not clearly established based on previous research. A participant emphasized a continuous process prevalent in common higher education institutions, where data validity subsequently impacts the trustworthiness of the information provided for students' learning and outcomes. Generally speaking, LA enables faculty members to enhance teaching.

Research findings revealed that customized teaching pedagogies must be enhanced to better match with the PLOs and CLOs of MQA. One issue highlighted here is that lecturers must give appropriate input to "technology", as the participant described that "technology is a dumb thing". Nonetheless, the guidelines of LA should be included in QA standards, as the output of QA is measured by the QA framework.

As such, one significant impulse for conducting this research is to enhance the benchmark of Malaysia's education standard to a greater height in terms of performance of students as a whole. The issue subsequently is whether we are just meeting the benchmark or simultaneously participating in a number of games that hold the institution accountable. Having said that, are we delivering a transactional job to fulfill what is enforced by the government, or are we driven by a passion to be a true educationalist for its purpose? This in turn raises doubts among participants as to whether we do really want to do it, and if so, in which area do we want to do it.

6.3.5.3 Key Risks

The objective of all educators is to guarantee that students acquire the ability to make informed decisions and excel in their endeavors. Students cultivate not only individual competencies but also societal skills; this entails the enhancement of social consciousness, fostering an understanding of societal dynamics and the organization of knowledge in relation to collective and individual well-being, alongside human rights and responsibilities. (Granados, 2015).

Serious questions normally asked by parents and students are, "where to learn knowledge needed?" and "what is the quality of learning and operations at universities?" The rapid advancement of technology complicates sustainability efforts, imposing additional pressure to ensure that selected tools enhance learning outcomes in measurable ways. This is crucial for aligning needs with limited resources and maintaining QA, particularly concerning the relevance of knowledge acquired for the industry. In this instance, five principal dangers have developed, encompassing data relevance, resistance to change, transformational change obstacles, and breaches of data rights.

Participants in this case study shared the thoughts query: "Is LA relevant, and where is the data?" As mentioned earlier with regard to the response of a participant on the limitation on future skills, in this case, LA is only relevant to the present world. In addition, participants representing stakeholders in this case study highlighted the availability of data, not just current data but also pre-entry data of students. This is supported by Berry (2017), whose findings indicate that age and educational level are important to ensure success in LA intervention. The issue of resistance to change is again raised in this section, as most participants shared the same thoughts. As put forward by Scalter (2017) and Rick (2013) on LA's impact on job, findings also show reasons for staff include lack of self-management for improvement, lack of commitment and generic level of resistance to adoption of new technologies. As for students, the greatest fear is to be honest and transparent toward free speech, which is predominantly due to the culture of the community in Malaysia. Transformational change takes time, and it takes all in the institutions to be involved. One of the many contextual issues such as the support of government is critical in impacting international competitiveness. The way management addresses the trends has to be visionary and firm, as well as the culture of the institution, so that values of LA can be embedded for sustainability. This has been extensively discussed in the section on ethical issues. The breach of data rights has been giving much pressure to HEIs on both physical access and logical access, with the establishment of system security policy and guidelines of the institutions. Most participants shared the same thoughts on this issue, which was congruent with most findings put forward by Johnson (2017) and Hoel et al. (2017).

6.4 Conclusion

Points wrapped up in the previous chapters are well presented and explained in the 3S for the LA model of QA:

- LA matters to students in their learning processes and learning outcomes. That includes facilitating student interaction with lecturers by utilizing and analyzing data on prior knowledge and learning styles, thereby reducing knowledge gaps, accommodating students' learning paces, predicting learning trajectories, providing personalized learning experiences, aligning benchmarks with the curriculum, tracking data beyond mere statistics, and measuring non-cognitive skills. On the other hand, other important points on issues in learning outcomes are the ethical implications of the established benchmarks, the elements of outcomes that extend beyond mere grades, the acknowledgment that learning outcomes may be misinterpreted and consequently miscalculated, thereby affecting the perceived academic standards; inquiries into the meaning of grades, the notion that learning serves solely for knowledge acquisition, the necessity of incorporating student attitudes into grading, the distinction between learned and applied knowledge, the challenges posed by incompatible educational systems that yield divergent expectations for outcomes, the potential for cultural measurement of learning outcomes, the accuracy of generic attainment as a measure of success, and the resolution of issues related to knowledge transfer. Real-time feedback can bridge the gap of dropout rates due to failure.

- The highlights on the effort for the well-being of the students in the interest of management and faculties were discovered. This encompasses the early intervention system that aids students, enhances student outcomes, decreases attrition rates, provides guidance for policy formulation regarding the adoption of LA and implements a real-time feedback system that benefits both lecturers and students. Conversely, regarding the ethical adoption of LA, shareholders expressed a desire for the LA modeling to be objective, its processes to be transparent, data security concerns to be addressed and for appropriate policies and guidelines to be established. Additionally, issues related to human intervention suggest that generalizations in predictive outcomes may be misrepresented. Stakeholders identified several values of LA, including the effective acquisition of data through structured learning, the provision of accurate, immediate and essential information that might motivate students, and additional benefits derived from human engagement..
- Regarding the barriers, if the implementation of LA for viability of LA implementation toward achieving QA, the main points contributed include resistance to change, alignment of structure and practice to change, infrastructural support and impact on staff's job activities. Generally, the common perception of stakeholders studied includes lack of commitment and staff involvement; staff resistance to technology regardless of age, technology savvy or otherwise, or level of passion for their, whether it is fulfilling or is merely transactional. The successful implementation of this change necessitates an understanding of the framework, the establishment of a timeline on this transformation and the provision of essential tools and platforms.
- Policies, procedures and practices and leadership practices are utmost critical factors in this research case study. Policies on transformation efforts impacting staff contribution to LA must be developed and adhered to, in addition to the technology support. Redesigning of staff duties and responsibilities is fundamental. Furthermore,, effective communication and top-down/bottom-up collaborative leadership are the most critical success factors. Nevertheless, distributed leadership, as explained in this case study, is a perspective in thinking, not hard rules to be followed.

- AI is transforming education by working with established learning theories in recent years. Research studies show that AI can analyze student activities to predict learning success (i.e., cognitivism) and personalize learning experiences (i.e., constructivism). AI offers support such as personalized learning and improved decision-making through LA. While AI holds great potential, special attention is to be given to ethical considerations with respect to data privacy, bias and faculty readiness. Ultimately, further research is needed to fully harness the power of AI and LA for personalized learning and educational improvement.

References

Bates, A. W. (2015). Teaching in a digital age – Guidelines for designing teaching and learning. *Creative commons attribution-non-commercial 4.0 international license.* https://bccampus.ca/open-textbook-project/

Berry, L. J. (2017). *Using learning analytics to predict academic success in online and face-to-face learning environment.* https://scholarworks.boisestate.edu/cgi/viewcontent.cgi?article=2317&context=td#page64

Bolden, R. (2011). Distributed leadership in organizations: A review of theory and research. *International Journal of Management Review*, *13*, 251–219. https://doi.org/10.1111/j.1468-2370.2011.003060x

Bolden, R., Petrov, G., & Gosling, J. (2009). Distributed leadership in higher education. *Educational Management Administration & Leadership*, *37*(2), 257–277. SAGE Publications. https://doi.org/10.1177/1741143208100301

Buyarski, C., Murray, J., & Torstrick, R. (2017). Learning analytics across a statewide system. In J. Zilvinskis & V. Boarder (Eds.), *Learning analytics in higher education. New directions for higher education, 179* (Fall). Jossey-Bass.

Campbell, J. P., DeBlois, P. B., & Oblinger, D. G. (2007). Academic analytics: A new tool for a new era. *EDUCASE Review*, *42*(4).

Clow, D. (2012). The learning analytics cycle: Closing the loop. In D. Gasevic & S. Buckingham Shum (Eds.), *Proceedings from the 2nd international learning analytics and knowledge conference* (p. 1340138). ACM. http://doi.org/10.1145/2330601.2330636

Diamond, J. B., & Spillane, J. P. (2016). School leadership and management from a distributed perspective: A 2016 retrospective and prospective. *Management in Education*, *30*(4), 147–154.

Dix, A., & Leavesley, J. (2015). *Learning analytics for the academics: An action perspective.* http://alandix.com/academic/papers/JUCS-action-analytics-2015/jucs_action_analytics-2015.pdf

Elmes, J. (2017). *Six significant challenges for technology in higher education in 2017.* https://www.timeshighereducation.com/features/six-significant-challenges-technology-higher-education-2017

Gasevic, D., Dawson, S., & Pardo, A. (2016). How do we start? State and directions of learning analytics adoption. *International council for open and distance education.* http://icde.memberclicks.net/assets/RESOURCES/dragan_la_report%20cc%20licence.pdf

Gosling, J., & Bolden, R. (2009). Distributed leadership in higher education: What does IT accomplish? *Leadership*, *5*(3), 299–310. https://doi.org/10.1177/1742715009337762

Granados, J. (2015). *The challenges of higher education in the 21st century*. http://www.guninetwork.org/articles/challenges-higher-education-21st-century

Harris, A., & Spillane, J. (2008). Distributed leadership through the looking glass. *Management in Education*, *22*(1), 31–34. https://doi.org/10.1177/0892020607085623

Hoel, T., & Chen, W. (2016). Implications of the European data protection regulations for learning analytics design. In *Presentation at the international workshop on learning analytics and educational data mining (LAEDM 2016) om conjunction with the international conference on collaboration technologies (CollabTech2016), Kanazawa, Japan, September 14–16*. http://www.hoel.nu/files/LAEDM_KAnazawa_Sep2016_Hoel_Chen_final_w_header.pdf

Hoel, T., Griffiths, D., & Chen, W. (2017). The Influence of data protection and privacy frameworks on the design of learning analytics system. *LAK. Proceedings of the seventh international learning analytics & knowledge conference* (pp. 243–252). https://doi.org/10.1145/3027385.3027414

Johnson, J. A. (2017). Ethics and justice in learning analytics. In J. Zilvinskis & V. Boarder (Eds.), *Learning analytics in higher education. New directions for higher education, 179* (Fall) (pp. 77–87). Jossey-Bass.

Knight, S., & Shum, S. B. (2013). Chapter 1: Theory and learning analytics. In *Handbook of learning analytics*, Connected Intelligence Center. University of Technology Sydney. https://doi.org/10.18608/hla17.001.

Knight, S., Shum, S. B., & Littleton, K. (2014). Epistemology, assessment, pedagogy: Where learning meets analytics in the middle space. *Journal of Learning Analytics*, *1*(2). http://epress.lib.uts.edu.au/journals/index.php/JLA/article/view/3538

Lim. (2021). *Learning analytics towards achieving quality assurance: A case study of private university in Kuala Lumpur* [Unpublished doctoral dissertation, University Malaya, Kuala Lumpur].

Lonn, S., Krumm, A. E., Waddington, R. J., & Teasley, S. D. (2012). Bridging the gap from knowledge to action: Putting analytics in the hands of academic advisors. *LAK'12 proceedings of the 2nd international conference on learning analytics and knowledge*. New York.

Malaysian Qualifications Agency. (2017). *Malaysian qualification framework (MQF)* (2nd ed.). http://pps.utem.edu.my/phocadownloadpap/2018%20MQF%202nd%20Edition%2002042018.pdf

Malaysian Qualifications Agency. (2018a). *Code of Practice for Programme Accreditation* (2nd ed.). Retrieved from https://www2.mqa.gov.my/qad/garispanduan/COPPA/2019/Oct/26092019%20CLEAN%20COPPA%202nd%20Edition%20(2017).pdf

Malaysian Qualifications Agency. (2018b). *COPIA form: MQA-03 (Self-Review Portfolio)* (2nd ed.). Retrieved from http://www.mqa.gov.my/portalMQAv3/borang/copia/MQA-03

Ministry of Higher Education. (2015). *Malaysia education blueprint 2015–2025 (higher education)* (Malaysia, Ministry of Higher Education, Putrajaya). Ministry of Higher Education. https://www.um.edu.my/docs/

default-source/about-um_document/media-centre/um-magazine/4-executive-summary-pppm-2015-2025.pdf?sfvrsn=

Mitchell, R. K., Agle, B. R., & Wood, D. J. (1997). *Towards a theory of stakeholder identification and salience: Defining the principle of who and what really counts*. http://www.jstor.org/stable/pdfplus/259247.pdf

Namoun, A., & Alshanqiti, A. (2021). Predicting student performance using data mining and learning analytics techniques: A systematic literature review. *Applied Sciences*, *11*(1), 237. https://doi.org/10.3390/app11010237

Nissenbaum, H. (2010). *Privacy in context: Technology, policy, and the integrity of social life*. Stanford Law Books.

Pistilli, M. D. (2017). Leaner analytics and student success interventions. In J. Zilvinskis & V. Boarder (Eds.), *Learning analytics in higher education. New directions for higher education, 179* (Fall). Jossey-Bass.

Pistilli, M. D., & Arnold, K. E. (2010). Purdue signals: Mining real-time academic data to enhance student success. *About Campus*, *15*(3), 22–24. Thousand Oaks California.

Rick, T. (2013). *Resistant to change is a problem*. https://www.torbenrick.eu/blog/change-management/change-is-not-the-problem-resistance-to-change-is-the-problem/

Scalter, N. (2017). Learning analytics adoption and implementation plan. *Effective Learning Analytic*. https://analytics.jiscinvolve.org/wp/2017/03/21/learning-analytics-adoption-and-implementation-trends

Sclater, N., & Mullan, J. (2017). *Jisc briefing: Learning analytics and student success – assessing the evidence*. https://repository.jisc.ac.uk/6560/1/learning-analytics_and_student_success.pdf

Simmons, J. M. (2011). *A national study of student early alert models at four-year institutions of higher education* [Doctoral dissertation]. ProQuest Dissertations and Thesis database (UMI 3482551).

Spillane, J. P. (2005). Distributed leadership. *The Educational Forum*, *69*(2), 143–150. https://doi.org/10.1080/00131720508984678.

Spillane, J. P., & Diamond, J. B. (2007). A distributed perspective on and in practice. In J. P. Spillane & J. B. Diamond (Eds.), *Distributed leadership in practice* (pp. 146–166). Teachers College Press.

Spillane, J. P., Halverson, R., & Diamond, J. (2004). Towards theory of leadership practice: A distributed perspective. *Journal of Curriculum Studies*, *36*(1), 3–34. https://doi.org/10.1080/0022027032000106726.

Srikanthan, G., & Dalrymple, J. F. (2002). Developing a holistic model for quality in higher education. *Quality in Higher Education*, *8*(3), 215–224. https://doi.org/10.1080/1353832022000031656. https://pdfs.semanticscholar.org/e6ec/9e984214bab5b298488f41442a095660ffd1.pdf?_ga=2.209295131.843471868.1540443894-1757868047.1540443894

Tam, A. C. F. (2018). Conceptualizing distributed leadership: Diverse voices of positional leaders in early childhood education. *Leadership and Policy in Schools*. https://doi.org/10.1080/15700763.2018.1513156

Thille, C., & Zimmaro, D. (2017). Incorporating learning analytics in the classroom. In J. Zilvinskis & V. Boarder (Eds.), *Learning analytics in higher education. New directions for higher education, 179* (Fall). Jossey-Bass.

Wagner, E., & Longajecker, D. (2016). Scaling student success with predictive analytics: Reflections after four years in the data trenches. *Change, 48*(1), 52–58.

Wan, S. W.-Y. (2014) Distributed leadership in higher education: Hong Kong academics' perceptions and practices. In A. Kwan, E. Wong, T. Kwong, P. Lau & A. Goody (Eds.), *Research and development in higher education: Higher education in a globalized world, 37* (pp. 323–341). https://www.researchgate.net/profile/Sally_Wan/publication/303570054_Distributed_leadership_in_higher_education_Hong_Kong_academics%27_perceptions_and_practices/links/5748ff5d08ae2e0dd30169d3/Distributed-leadership-in-higher-education-Hong-Kong-academics-perceptions-and-practices.pdf?origin=publication_detail

West, D., Luzeckyj, A., Tasir, Z., & Toohey, D. P. (2018). Learning analytics experience among academics in Australia and Malaysia: A comparison. *Australian Journal of Educational Technology, 34*(3), 122–139. https://doi.org/10.14742ajet.3836

Williams, M. K. (2017). John Dewey in the 21st century. *Journal of Inquiry & Action in Education, 9*(1), 91–102. Retrieved from https://digitalcommons.buffalostate.edu/jiae/vol9/iss1/7

Wong, T. M. B. (2017). Learning analytics in higher education: Analysis in case studies. *Asia Association of Open Universities Journal, 12*(1), 21–40. https://doi.org/10.1108/AAOUJ-01-2017-0009

Zhou, M., & Lin, W. (2016). Adaptability and life satisfaction: The moderating role of social support. *Frontiers in Psychology, 7*(1134). https://doi.org/10.3389/fpsyg.2016.01134. https://www.ncbi.nlm.nih.gov/pmc/articles/PMC4963457/

Zilvinskis, J., & Boarder, V. (2017). *Learning analytics in higher education. New directions for higher education, 179* (Fall). Jossey-Bass.

Index

Note: Page numbers in *italics* indicate a figure and page numbers in **bold** indicate a table on the corresponding page.

For Product Safety Concerns and Information please contact our EU representative GPSR@taylorandfrancis.com
Taylor & Francis Verlag GmbH, Kaufingerstraße 24, 80331 München, Germany

www.ingramcontent.com/pod-product-compliance
Lightning Source LLC
LaVergne TN
LVHW010934110826
845149LV00013B/2595

* 9 7 8 1 0 3 2 9 5 3 6 5 6 *